"How to Survive and Thrive In the Merchant Services Industry"

Co-Authored by Marc J. Beauchamp And William Graham

©Performance Training Systems

"Our mission is to provide cutting-edge tools, education and consulting services to provide our customers a true competitive advantage"

Copyright© 2003 Performance Training Systems

All rights reserved. No part of this book may be used or reproduced in any manner whatsoever without the written permission of the Publisher. Printed in the United States of America. For information email: marcb@surviveandthrive.biz

ISBN: 0-9741884-0-9

Printed in the U.S.A

FIRST EDITION

Acknowledgements

We'd like to thank everyone that had a part in the development and production of this book, especially our interview participants, our editor - Roger Leslie, and graphics artist - Robert Hendrix. We'd like to extend a special thank you to Cynthia Dorrill editor of Transaction World Magazine for her assistance and valuable input.

We understand that time is a precious commodity and you were willing to spend yours on helping us with this project.

And finally to our family and friends for putting up with the late nights and weekend marathons, without your support nothing is possible.

About the Authors

Marc Beauchamp is a dynamic and engaging entrepreneur who has developed several successful companies. He has over 15 years experience in sales, training and marketing in various roles. In addition to merchant services, he has sold payroll systems, human resource management solutions, computer software and hardware, website design services and an array of financial and insurance products.

He has served in multiple capacities, including Account Executive, National Account Manager, Sales Manager, Marketing Director, Vice President and CEO.

He has worked in the merchant services industry since 1996. Marc has hired and trained several thousand merchant services professionals. At one point he managed a full time outside sales force of 80 representatives, an inside sales force of 25, and an office staff of 8 with national offices in most major cities in the United States.

©Performance Training Systems

In 2002 alone he provided consulting and training for over 500 bankcard sales representatives. He is uniquely aware of the challenges facing field sales representatives, sales managers, Issuers, Acquirers and ISOs.

Marc is a certified NLP instructor and now speaks, trains and conducts consulting for the merchant services industry through Performance Training Systems.

Performance Training Systems is a company dedicated to providing cutting edge tools, education and consulting services to give their customers a true competitive advantage.

Marc lives in Houston, Texas with his wife and three daughters.

William Graham is and has been a successful entrepreneur for over 44 years. William was born in Denver, Colorado, where he started his career at age 16. By the time he reached his 18th birthday he had become the youngest staff member for a fortune 500 company.

A charismatic visionary Mr. Graham has over 44 years of successful sales and marketing experience, with hands on experience in all aspects of the wholesale and retail product distribution industry. He has opened over 75 offices for nationally known companies such as TV fanfare, Technicolor, Serveomatic, Electroway, international coupons and many others.

In addition, he was responsible for product training, personal development, and sales and motivational seminars for these firms. He has set sales records that are unmatched today. He spent 22 years in the advertising industry. Mr. Graham has now been in the transaction processing business for over 10 years, and has been a successful ISO and MSP, Mr. Graham continues to do training seminars for the industry,

©Performance Training Systems

he feels that there is a growing need to combine the old with the new. With emphasis on old time closing techniques.

He now consults for many companies and has done training seminars on closing the sale in over 40 different ISO offices. Mr. Graham has conducted over 20 training seminars for 1st national processing and iPayment, Inc. He speaks and conducts training seminars, and continues to teach the old school. William is a member of Performance Training Systems. He lives in Southern California with his wife Peggy.

"When you are inspired by some great purpose, some extraordinary project, all your thoughts break their bonds; your mind transcends limitations, your consciousness expands in every direction, and you find yourself in a new, great and wonderful world. Dormant forces, faculties and talents become alive, and you discover yourself to be a greater person by far than you ever dreamed yourself to be."

- Patanjali

Table of Contents

Chapter 1: Why We Wrote This Book — 12

Section 1 - Industry Basics

Chapter 2: The Merchant Services Industry — 15
Chapter 3: Industry History — 19
Chapter 4: How the System is Designed — 43
Chapter 5: The Anatomy of a Credit Card — 50
Chapter 6: The Transaction Flow — 54
Chapter 7: Interchange — 61
Chapter 8: Typical Merchant Fees — 63
Chapter 9: Credit Card Disputes — 68
Chapter 10: Debit and Check Card Processing — 72
Chapter 11: Electronic Benefits Transfer — 75
Chapter 12: Check Processing — 77
Chapter 13: ACH Processing — 81
Chapter 14: Gift Cards — 84
Chapter 15: Loyalty Cards — 86
Chapter 16: Smart Cards — 88
Chapter 17: Custom Card Applications — 92
Chapter 18: Wireless Processing — 93
Chapter 19: MCommerce — 96
Chapter 20: ECommerce — 98
Chapter 21: Processing Equipment — 102
Chapter 22: Leasing — 105
Chapter 23: Other Tier II Products — 108
Chapter 24: Consumer Fraud — 112

Section 2 – Sales Techniques

Chapter 25: Selling In The Merchant Services Industry — 125
Chapter 26: Where The Money Is — 127

Chapter 27:	What's Your Strategy	132
Chapter 28:	Target Marketing	134
Chapter 29:	The Extraordinary Salesperson	136
Chapter 30:	7 Reasons Salespeople Fail	140
Chapter 31:	The Sales Process	144
Chapter 32:	Prospecting	145
Chapter 33:	The Science of Rapport	163
Chapter 34:	Analyzing Needs and Uncovering Buying Values	172
Chapter 35:	The Presentation	177
Chapter 36:	Why Do People Buy?	184
Chapter 37:	Preventing Objections	187
Chapter 38:	What Benefits Do You Offer?	189
Chapter 39:	Gaining Commitment	192
Chapter 40:	Lets Talk About Price	200
Chapter 41:	Follow Up	205

Section 3 – Personal Development

Chapter 42:	Time Management 101	207
Chapter 43:	What Is Your Time Worth	210
Chapter 44:	Tips to Organize Your Time	212
Chapter 45:	Goal Setting	214
Chapter 46:	Motivation 101	217

Section 4 – Industry Interviews

Interview with David J. Bartone	222
Interview with Bob Carr	237
Interview with Mary Dees	240
Interview with Cynthia Dorrill	244
Interview with Mary Gerdts	248
Interview with Paul Green	250
Interview with Gil Gillis	254
Interview with Lee Ladd	257
Interview with Paul Martaus	260

Section 5 – Appendices

Appendix A:	Income Goal Sheet	267
Appendix B:	Daily Call Sheet	268
Appendix C:	Developing a Telemarketing Script	270
Appendix D:	Sample Questionnaire	273
Appendix E:	Pain and Pleasure Exercise	275
Appendix F:	Preventing Objections Worksheet	276
Appendix G:	Advertising 101	278
Appendix H:	Industry Internet Resources	287
Appendix I:	Tools You Can Use	291

Section 6 – Industry Glossary

Industry Glossary	294
Commonly Used Acronyms	318
Bibliography	320

©Performance Training Systems

► Chapter One ◄

Why We Wrote This Book

With over 20 years of combined experience in the bankcard industry and after working with multiple ISOs and financial institutions we came to the realization that there never had been an industry guidebook for field salespeople. We wanted to create a book that covered everything from basic industry information to traditional sales techniques and new sales strategies.

I remember the first company I went to work for (Marc B), they trained me for one hour in a coffee shop, gave me some brochures and said "Go Get'm Tiger". I was one of the lucky ones; I actually made it. But I've seen hundreds of salespeople leave this industry because the time was not taken educate them properly.

There was no roadmap or material that provided a general overview of the merchant services industry or explained how everything really worked, let alone something that would help me develop and execute a sales plan.

Even today there is a significant gap in the skill level of the merchant services salesperson. Other industries, such as telecommunications, computer services, financial investment products, loan origination and real estate, offer in-depth training and industry information for their salespeople.

But, the merchant services arena has not, until now. The agent out in the field is often left to his own devices. This creates an uneducated salesperson that projects a negative image for the ISO, Acquirer, Member Bank, Associations and the Industry as a whole.

Our goal is to stop this madness and help you become a knowledgeable, creative, professional salesperson. In this book, we will educate, motivate and empower merchant service professionals to better represent their companies, the industry and themselves in a more informed and ethical manner.

You'll find a history of the industry, how the system works, basic explanations about rates and fees and descriptions about existing and future products. You will also find valuable information and interviews about industry trends and product development, as well as a step-by-step approach to prospecting, lead development and the sales process.

There is a difference between knowing "About" something and truly "Knowing" something. If I tell you how to ride a bike you will know "About" riding a bike. But you won't really "Know" how to ride a bike until you get on it and pedal. We know how to sell merchant services; there are a lot of people that know "About" the business. We've taken our lumps for sure and hopefully our experience will help you avoid some of the "bumps in the road" we've experienced.

Like any book, this will continue to be a work in progress. We welcome any comments on how we can make this a better guide for new and experienced salespeople.

Please email comments, suggestions or ideas to Marc Beauchamp at:

marcb@surviveandthrive.biz

▶ Chapter Two ◀

The Merchant Services Industry

The merchant services industry is a dynamic, ever-changing business. New regulations, technological advancements and competitive pressures keep the excitement level high, to say the least.

What is our industry called? I've heard many names for the business including the Bankcard Industry, Merchant Processing Industry, Transaction Processing Industry, Payment Processing Industry, The Financial Services Industry, The Electronic Transaction Industry, and The Credit Card Industry.

Whatever name you want to call it, we are in the same business as every other company on the planet; serving our customer – the merchant.

Without the merchant we have no industry. Our purpose in this endeavor is to add value to the merchant so he can add value to his customer. We do this by offering a variety of products and services. The following is a breakdown of the most common products offered in our industry. We have distinguished them into three groups: Core Product, Tier I Products and Tier II Products.

Core Product:

- **Credit Card Processing**
    - **Retail**
    - **Card Not Present**
    - **Wireless**

- Internet
- High Risk

Tier I Products:

- **Debit Processing**
    - Online/Offline
    - ATM
    - EBT

- **Check Processing:**
    - Electronic Check Conversion
    - Check Guarantee
    - Check Verification
    - Online Check Processing
    - Check Imaging
    - ACH Processing

Tier II Products

- **Biometrics**
- **Loyalty Card Programs**
- **Pre Paid Products**
    - Gift Cards
    - Debit Cards
    - Phone Cards
    - Cellular
    - Internet
    - Home Phone

- **Custom Applications**
    - Payroll Cards
    - Smart Card Applications

- Government ID
- Mass Transit
- Parking Systems
- Healthcare
  - Benefits Verification
  - Electronic Claims Processing
- Information Security
- Banking

- Medical Applications
- Age Verification
- Identification Products
- Time and Attendance
- Closed Loop Applications

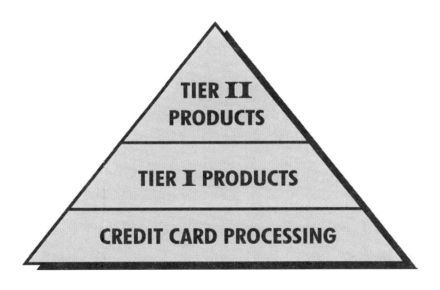

Credit card processing is the foundation of our product offering, in the majority of cases we will build upon this core product. This is the one service that retail and Internet merchants require if they want to succeed in business.

Tier I products such as debit, EBT (Electronic Benefits Transfer) and check processing are secondary products that appeal to a large percentage of retail merchants.

Tier II products are more specialized in nature and provide specific benefits to certain types of merchants. Many times you can lead with a Tier II product in order to acquire their credit card processing business.

We will discuss these products in the following chapters, but before we get into the business lets take a look at where we have been.

► Chapter Three ◄

Industry History

The credit business has a long history; it was first used in Assyria, Babylon and Egypt 3,000 years ago. The bill of exchange was established in the 14th century. Debts were settled by one-third cash and two-thirds bill of exchange. Paper money followed in the 17th century.

The first advertisement for credit was placed in 1730 by Christopher Thornton, who offered furniture that could be bought over time.

From the 18th century until the early part of the 20th, tallymen sold clothes in return for small weekly payments. They were called "tallymen" because they kept a record or tally of what people had bought on a wooden stick. One side of the stick was marked with notches to represent the amount of debt and the other side was a record of payments.

In 1914 Western Union issued a metal plate or "card" to their employees in lieu of a paycheck. This card was only good for purchases within the company owned stores. While not very favorable by today's standards, it was still the first "card." However, the system was "closed" - meaning no one other than the company participated.

A bankcard system is considered an "open" system, all its members can participate.

The following is a timeline of the credit card industry:

1950

- Diners Club/Carte Blanche® introduced the first Travel and Entertainment Card.

    The designation Travel and Entertainment ("T&E") was due to the intended cardholder's use because it was designed to relieve a businessman from having to take cash on the road and to provide for his travel and entertainment expenses.

    Diner's Club is also considered the first acquirer because they were the first to charge merchants a discount rate. The discount rate is a percentage taken from each sale accepted as a fee to the acquirer/issuer.

- The "Charg-It" system helped introduce the first bank credit card, which was circulated by Franklin National Bank of Long Island, New York in 1951.

    Once an application was submitted for credit worthiness, a card was issued. Merchants copied information from the card onto a sales slip and called for an approval for each transaction over a specified limit. The bank would then credit the merchant's account for the sale, less a discount to cover the cost for providing the loan.

1958

- Bank of America, based in San Francisco, California, launched its blue, white and gold BankAmericard.

    With the entire state of California as its market, the card was an early success, and it's the first "revolving-credit" card with universal merchant acceptance, allowing cardholders the option of paying their account balances in installments with a monthly finance charge applied to the remaining balance.

- American Express enters the industry and issues its first card.

  Marketed for travel and entertainment use too, it along with Diner's Club became known as T&E Cards.

1959

Many financial institutions had begun credit programs. Simultaneously card issuers offered the added services of revolving credit.

This gave cardholders the choice to either pay off their balance or maintain a balance and pay a finance charge.

1966

- Bank of America expanded its bankcard program by forming the BankAmericard Service Corporation, licensing banks outside of California to issue cards to their customers.

  Because the cost of bankcard programs is shared among its Member financial institutions, even small banks across the country were able to join.

  As BankAmericard was introduced, other banks began looking for new ways to compete.

- Also in 1966, 14 banks formed the Interbank Card Association (ICA), a new association with the ability to exchange information on credit card transactions.

- The following year, four California banks opened their memberships to other financial institutions in the Western U.S. (Western States Bankcard Association).

  Their product was known as MasterCharge. They purchased the right to use this name from First National Bank of Louisville (currently known as National City Bank of Kentucky).

- The Western States Bankcard Association (WSBA) licenses the Interbank Card Association (ICA) to use the MasterCharge name and Logo.

  By the late 1960's, to compete with BankAmericard, numerous financial institutions become MasterCharge members.

1968

- Interbank Card Association (ICA) began a huge global network by forming an association with Banco Nacional in Mexico.

  Later that year, they formed an alliance in Europe with Eurocard.

  The first Japanese members also joined that year.

1969

- Most regional banks converted their independent programs to either BankAmericard or Master Charge.

- Master Charge sold to California Bank Association.

1970

- BankAmericard transferred control and ownership of the BankAmericard program to the banks that issued the cards, forming National BankAmericard Inc. (NBI).

  At this time, more than 1,400 banks offered either BankAmerica or MasterCharge credit cards.

- Worthern Bank & Trust Co., Little Rock, AR, took NBI to court claiming NBI's exclusive membership conditions (issuing) placed Worthern Bank at competitive disadvantage for signing up merchants.

  Worthern lost the first case and the initial appeal.

  However, when Worthern Bank threatened to take the NBI case to the Supreme Court, NBI (in response to the U.S. Department of Justices' opinion and recommendation) changed its rules to allow dual membership for U.S. members.

  MasterCharge followed and adopted a similar policy. This policy would become known as "Duality" and forever changed the industry going forward.

1970's

The paper-based system became cumbersome. Losses and tremendous overhead were two major problems. The need for automation pushes both associations to find a better way to handle transactions.

So, both National Bankamericard and MasterCharge introduced electronic payment systems in two stages.

1st Stage

- In 1973, the authorization system is re-vamped. Authorization is the process of assuring that adequate credit is available on the card and capturing that "authorized" amount to reduce the available credit. Previously this was based on a merchant specific floor limit and a phone call was placed to a call center for any amount over the floor limit.

- MasterCharge introduced INAS (InterBank National Authorization System) for "on-line" authorizations the same year.

- MasterCharge also introduced the world's first on-line global electronic card authorization system, *Base I (Service Exchange Authorization System)* which reduced the time consumers needed to wait for authorization from more than five minutes to less than one minute.

Authorization was now available 24 hours a day.

2nd Stage, 1974

- NBI introduced *Base II (Exchange and Clearing Systems)* for on-line electronic clearing and settlement.

- Bank of America's international licensees chartered an international company, IBANCO, to administer BankAmericard, Inc. outside the U.S.

©Performance Training Systems

- MasterCharge introduced INET (Interbank Network for Electronic Transfer) for clearance and settlement.

Early to mid 70's

Many other countries joined the Interbank Card Association (ICA) and by the late 1970s, ICA has members from as far as Africa and Australia.

1974

- International Bankcard Company (IBANCO) is formed to administer the BankAmericard program internationally.

  The card encountered some resistance because its name is identified too closely with the U.S. and the Bank of America.

1975

- National BankAmericard Inc. (NBI) introduces the first national deposit access card, enabling cardholders to debit charges from their deposit accounts rather than having charges posted lines of credit.

1976

- BankAmericard changes its name to Visa®, a simple, memorable name with an international flavor that is pronounced the same way in almost every language.

- NBI is renamed Visa U.S.A. and IBANCO is changed to Visa International®.

- The first bank becomes a dual member of both Associations, the result of the duality agreement 6 years earlier.

1979

- Visa introduced the first electronic dial terminal at the point of sale, which allows for much speedier purchase transactions.

- This led the way to electronic data capture (EDC) point-of-sale terminals, which virtually eliminated the time-consuming process of paper deposits.

- To reflect the commitment to international growth, ICA changes its name to MasterCard®.

1981

- MasterCard introduces the first gold bankcard program.

1982

- Visa issued their first premium card — Visa Premier® — to provide new kinds of services for upscale customers.

1983

- MasterCard is the first to use the laser hologram as an antifraud device.

- Visa launches the world's first global ATM network, providing 24-hour cash access to cardholders around the world and contributing to the convenience of modern business and leisure travel.

1984

- The rapid growth of the industry in the mid-80s leads to a rise in credit card fraud and counterfeiting.

- Visa establishes the Visa Risk Identification Service®, the first computer-based system to pinpoint suspicious card transactions at merchant locations.

1985-1988

Visa sales volume doubled.

1986

Globally, Visa becomes the first payment card system to offer multiple-currency clearing and settlement, providing financial institutions with faster methods of restitution and greatly increasing the efficiency of international transactions.

1987

- A MasterCard card becomes the first payment card issued in the People's Republic of China.

- Visa established the first computerized card transaction processing network in China.

©Performance Training Systems

1989

- MasterCard introduced the first bankcard with a tamper-resistant signature panel.

1990

- MasterCard unveiled a co-branding strategy and became the industry's co-branding leader.

1991

- MasterCard, in partnership with Europay International, launched Maestro®, the world's first truly global online debit program.

1991

- Maestro completed the first-ever coast-to-coast national online debit transaction in the United States.

1993

- Visa is the first to apply state-of-the-art neural network technologies to payments, thus greatly reducing the incidence of card fraud by giving Visa Member banks smarter and timelier data about suspicious transactions. By analyzing typical card usage patterns, the neural network-based risk management tool invented by Visa immediately notifies banks so they can inform their customers if a card appears to have been used by someone other than the legitimate cardholder. Visa offers the first international pre-paid card, Visa Travel Money. This allows travelers to put a set amount of money on their card in one currency and access that account while traveling in other countries, enhancing the safety and convenience of international travel and currency exchanges. Visa issues the first smart card that allows cardholders to accumulate merchant loyalty points by making purchases on their payment cards. Visa becomes the first to offer a suite of corporate, business and purchasing cards to accommodate the needs of business of all sizes.

1995

- Visa co-develops industry-wide chip card specifications, Europay/Visa/MasterCard (EVM), to ensure that all chip cards will operate with all chip-reading terminals, regardless of location, financial institution, or manufacturer. As a result, smart credit cards and debit cards are now standardized to the point where cardholders can confidently use their chip cards to access their accounts from any EMV terminal worldwide.

1996

- MasterCard Global Service® became the first program to provide cardholders with telephone access to core emergency and special services in 21 languages, from 130 countries (today, in 196 countries and 46 languages).

- MasterCard contracted with AT&T to replace its transaction network infrastructure with the industry's first virtual private network design, which delivers faster response time and lower costs.

1997

- The first SET 1.0 (Secure Electronic Transaction) purchase using a smart card is completed. This technology, co-developed by Visa, provides a high level of privacy, security, and authentication for payment card transactions made over the Internet. Visa announces the prototype for the first contactless commuter-cash smart card. Contactless terminals do not need a card to be physically inserted into the terminal and offer greater convenience and flexibility to cardholders.

- MasterCard acquired a 51% stake in Mondex International, which offers the only electronic-cash product that is globally interoperable, with a multicurrency capability.

- MasterCard was the first payments organization to cap uniform liability limits for unauthorized use at US$50 for all United States.

1998

- MasterCard/Cirrus® ATM Network expands to Antarctica.

- MasterCard and MYCAL Card Company in Japan announce the world's first migration from traditional credit cards to multi-application chip cards using the MULTOS™ operating systems.

- Visa, together with Standard Chartered Bank, introduces the world's first multi-application smart card based on open standards-based technology. As a result, it becomes more cost-effective for banks to offer multi-application cards that enable consumers to access multiple financial accounts and other types of services - all on a single card. For example, debit accounts, lines of credit, stored value accounts as well as secure Internet shopping or merchant loyalty programs can now all be stored on one card.

1999

- Mondex™ e-cash and MULTOS became the first commercial products ever to receive the highest assurance level possible under the prestigious ITSEC (Information Technology Security Evaluation Criteria) security rating.

- The first online purchase of a U.S. Treasury Bond was made with a MasterCard card.

- Globally, Visa becomes the first to process 25 billion consumer payment transactions per year. Visa is the first payment association to promote a global infrastructure for smart cards across multiple industries as a founding member of Global Platform, Inc. Visa conducts the world's first euro transaction using a payment card in the European Union. Visa joins the Wireless Application Protocol (WAP) Forum to develop standards for wireless delivery. Visa completes the first download of electronic cash via mobile phone that are powered by the GSM (Global Systems and Mobile Phone) network in Leeds, UK. Visa announces a pilot program with Nokia and MeritaNordbanken of Finland enabling cardless payments via mobile phones at both physical merchants and on the Internet. Visa, together with Citibank and the General Services Administration, introduces the world's most sophisticated, multi-application smart card. It is the first smart card to combine credit, employee identification, access control and biometric verification.

2000

- MasterCard became the first in the industry to establish a U.S. rule of no liability for the consumer from the unauthorized use of payment cards.

- Visa reaches a key milestone with one billion cards in use. Visa announces an enhanced Consumer Zero Liability Policy, which was originally launched in 1997. The new rule virtually eliminates consumer liability in cases of Visa card fraud over the Visa system, including Internet transactions. Under the previous policy, cardholders could be held liable for up to $50 if their credit or debit cards were fraudulently used on the Visa system, and they failed to report theft or unauthorized use within two business days. The new policy does not cover commercial card transactions.

- On April 3, 2000 Visa International moved its systems and processing services division into a wholly owned subsidiary company, named Inovant. Inovant provides global transaction processing for Visa. Smart Visa, a multi-function chip product, is launched in the United States. Visa Buxx is launched to open an underserved market of teenaged consumers and offer parents a tool to teach their teens about responsible money management. Visa U.S.A. announces Direct Exchange, which paves the way for a new generation of payment capabilities. Holiday spending volume on Visa credit and check cards between November 24 and December 29, 2000, reaches $101 billion. Online spending more than doubles over the past year. Visa U.S.A. launches it's national consumer education program, Practical Money Skills for Life which is aimed at helping high school students learn better money management skills.

2001

- MasterCard launches mc^2 Card, the first non-rectangular card.

- MasterCard becomes the first payments association to actively support all smart card platforms, enabling members to issue MasterCard, Maestro and Cirrus branded smart cards on MULTOS, JavaCard, or proprietary platforms.

- Visa completes the world's first secure payment transaction using a Palm™ handheld computer. Palm and Visa have worked with terminal manufacturers Ingenico and Verifone to enable the secure transfer of payment information from a Palm handheld to a Verifone or Ingenico point of sale payment terminal using infrared technology. Smart Visa Business cards, chip-enabled payment products tailored to the small business market, are launched in the United States.

2002

- MasterCard becomes the first bankcard association to convert to a private share corporation, in connection with its merger with Europay.

Today

Visa

- Visa has over 21,000 financial member institutions worldwide and is accepted at over 28 million locations in over 144 countries.

- VisaNet Processes over 3,700 transactions per second.

- Visa held 50.8% market share as 12/31/01.

- Visa combined credit and debit volume is $915.8 billion in the U.S. and $1.8 trillion worldwide.

- Visa had a total of 375 million cards issued as of first quarter of 2002. This included 259 million credit cards and 115 million check cards.

- The Visa check card has over 98 million cardholders who purchased over 158 billion worth of annual sales in 2000.

- The Visa Plus system of ATMs provides access to over 800,000 locations.

- There are more than 1 billion Visa, Visa Electron, Interlink, PLUS, and Visa Cash cards in the market today.

- Interlink has over 60 million cardholders.

Source: Visa, Retail Payments Research Project

MasterCard

- MasterCard's total dollar volume in 2002 was 1.14 trillion, an increase of 15.2% over 2001.

- MasterCard has over 25,000 member financial institutions in over 210 countries.

- MasterCard was accepted at over 30 million locations worldwide in 2002, an increase of 25.6% over 2001.

- The Maestro brand (MasterCard debit network) mark now appears on over 505.2 million cards worldwide.

- MasterCard held 37.1% market share as of 12/31/01.

- Maestro cardholders may access over 821,766 ATM locations.

- 4th quarter 2002 transactions increased by 13.2% over prior quarter for a total of 3.7 billion.

- By year-end 2002 MasterCard had issued 127 million branded smart cards.

Source: MasterCard, Retail Payments Research Project
Note: MasterCard is a trademark of MasterCard International Incorporated

©Performance Training Systems

American Express

1958

American Express® card, "Amex" is launched in the U.S. and Canada. As the company's background was in the travel business, the card was first accepted at restaurants and hotels. The company also successfully lobbied the Civil Aviation Board to enable airline travelers to purchase tickets with credit cards. By the end of the year, 253,000 American Express cards had been issued.

1959

Airlines, railroads and bus lines began accepting the card for payment. This was also the year that American Express introduced the industry's first plastic card. The company had 600,000 active cards by the end of 1959.

1960

Cruise lines started accepting American Express cards.

1962

Major oil companies start accepting Amex cards. With the addition of the oil companies, the card became a profitable division for the company for the first time. Also in 1962, American Express began providing detailed expense records on the back of charge receipts to help in substantiating records.

1965

American Express limits card member liability against fraudulent card use, an industry first.

1966

The company introduced its first premium card.

1972

Macy's becomes the first department store to accept the card, as do 36 Broadway theaters.

1987

American Express issues its first small business card.

Early 1990s

American Express launches the Everyday Savings program®, providing exclusive savings for small business customers. Today the program includes Dell, Exxon, Mobil, FedEx, Hertz, Hilton, and many more.

2000

American Express launches Blue for Business, one of the first smart cards issued in the United States.

Today

- As of 12/31/01, American Express held 4.7% of the U.S. card market.

- American Express Card members tend to spend more because they have more to spend.

- 45% of American households that earn over $50,000 have an American Express Card.

- American express had 55.2 million total cards in force by the end of 2001, up 7%. U.S. card base grew 4%.

- An American Express cardholder's average charge is 27% higher than their average charge on other cards.

- Incentive programs such as the Membership Rewards Program encourage Card members to use the American Express Card - 51% of Cardholders enrolled in the program go out of their way to use the card.

- 1.7 million companies (including almost 70% of the Fortune 500) use the American Express Corporate Card for business expenses.

Source: American Express, Visa Business Research study 12/31/01
Note: American Express is a registered trademark of the American Express Company

Diners Club

1949

Frank McNamara schedules a business meal at a New York restaurant called Major's Cabin Grill. Prior to dinner, he changes suits. After dinner, the waiter presents the bill. Frank reaches for his wallet . . . and realizes that he has left it in his other suit. McNamara finesses the situation, but that night he has a thought: Why should people be limited to spending what they are carrying in cash, instead of being able to spend what they can afford?

In February 1950, McNamara and his partner, Ralph Schneider, return to Major's Cabin Grill and order dinner. When the bill came, McNamara presents a small, cardboard card -- a Diners Club Card -- and signs for the purchase. In the credit card industry, this event is still known as the First Supper.

1950

Diners Club/Carte Blanche introduce the first Travel and Entertainment Card.

The designation Travel and Entertainment ("T&E") is due to the intended cardholder's use because it is designed to relieve a business man from having to take cash on the road and use for his travel and entertainment expenses.

"Charge-It" system helps introduce the first bank credit card, which is circulated by Franklin National Bank in Long Island, New York in 1951.

1955

Western Airlines is the first airline to accept the Diners Card. 10 years later every major domestic airline accepts the card.

1970's

Diners expands rapidly. Within 10 years Diners Club serves half of all fortune 500 companies.

1984

Diners Club creates Club Rewards, the industry's first relationship marketing program.

2000

Diners Club earns its third successive Freddie Award for "Best Affinity Charge Card Program."

Today

- Diners Club serves over 201 countries and more than 7 million merchants worldwide.

- Diners Club members charge 31 billion dollars in goods and services in 2001.

Source: Diners Club
Note: Dinners club is a registered trademark of Diners Club International, Ltd.

Discover Card

Originally introduced by Sears, Discover Financial Services is now a business unit of Morgan Stanley & Co. and operates the Discover Card® brand names.

Today

- For their fiscal year ending November 30, 2001, Discover had a net income of $726 million.

- Transaction volume hit a record of $93.3 billion, up 4% from 2000.

- Discover ads 721,000 new locations accepting the card, for a total of 4 million.

- Discover ads 4.8 million new accounts, bringing the total to 45.7 million account holders.

Source: Discover Card
Note: Discover Card is a registered trademark of Discover Financial Services, Inc.

The JCB International Credit Card

1961

Japan Credit Bureau (JCB®) is established in Japan.

1981

JCB enters the U.S. card merchant business.

©Performance Training Systems

1988

JCB International Credit Card Co., Ltd. established in Los Angeles.

1989

JCB formed a merchant business alliance with Bank of America.

1993

JCB Bank, N.A. established and launched a consumer credit card business in U.S.

1997

JCB launched their U.S. co-branded frequent flyer program "Northwest WorldPerks JCB Card."

Today

- JCB's worldwide cardholder base is 45 million.

- JCB is accepted at over 10 million locations worldwide with a sales volume of 42 billion dollars.

Source: jcbusa.com
Note: JCB is a registered trademark of JCB international credit card co., ltd.

► Chapter Four ◄

How the System is Designed

Visa and MasterCard are worldwide payment service organizations composed of member institutions. Thus, Visa and MasterCard are commonly referred to as bankcards. To become a member of Visa and MasterCard an organization must be a financial institution aka, a bank. The member bank may then be licensed to issue cards and/or acquire merchant transactions.

Member banks are required to provide cash advances on Visa and MasterCard cards at their teller windows. Member banks are issued a Bank Identification Number (BIN) and pay membership dues and assessments to the card associations.

Other cards such as American Express, Diners Club, Discover and JCB are also common in the electronic payment industry.

They are structured differently from Visa and MasterCard primarily in that they do not have "members" (member banks). They are self-contained companies that control issuing, acquiring, payment, fraud, rule setting and disputes.

Market share is also dramatically less for these "non-bankcards."

Visa and MasterCard do not:

- **Issue credit cards**
- **Establish criteria for evaluating applicants**
- **Set credit limits offered to cardholders**

©Performance Training Systems

- **Determine procedures for billing customers**

Visa and MasterCard are managers of their respective brands. As such, they:

- **Create advertising and promotion programs to support their brands**
- **Develop new products**
- **Conduct clearing and settlement processing of transactions (Interchange)**
- **Set and enforce rules and regulations governing the use and acceptance of their bankcards, such as operational procedures, interchange procedures, and graphic design approval of their cards.**

Member Banks/Issuers

Member banks are financial institutions that have entered into membership with Visa and/or MasterCard. The member bank must designate its intended use of the cards, either to issue these cards to consumers and/or to acquire new merchants.

Members can perform both of these activities or utilize other companies to perform services.

The issuer is responsible for the cardholder account program, which encompasses nearly all aspects of cardholder account activities ranging from acquiring new customers to billing current ones.

The Issuer's responsibilities include:

- **Acquisition and marketing of new accounts**
- **Processing applications, establishing credit limits and policies**
- **Overseeing design, manufacturing, and embossing of cards**
- **Handling of issuing and reissuing of cards**
- **Overseeing PIN numbers**
- **Maintaining authorization file**
- **Providing customer service**
- **Processing payments and handling settlement**
- **Establishing collections operations**

Managing a credit card program is expensive. Smaller banks can issue cards without becoming an issuing member by acting as an agent, which are called Agent Banks.

The issuer usually keeps most of the income from the cardholder account. The agent receives a small compensation for providing the application. This allows small banks to retain customers who want a credit card program.

Acquirer

The Acquirer is usually, but not always a member of Visa and MasterCard and contracts with merchants to accept merchant sales drafts, provides authorization terminals, direction, support, and the processing of merchant credit card transactions.

The key responsibilities of the Acquirer are:

- **Sales**
- **Fraud Investigation**
- **Pricing**

©Performance Training Systems

- **Merchant Acceptance**
- **Support Services**
- **Risk Management**

The acquirer charges a fee or "discount rate" for handling the transactions. The acquirer is registered with Visa and MasterCard and agrees to follow the association rules and regulations.

Examples of Acquirers are:

- **Chase Merchant Services**
- **National Processing Company**
- **Paymentech**
- **Nova**

Processor

The Processor is a company contracted by a member bank to authorize, capture, settle and clear transactions.

With the increasing costs of technology associated with electronic payments, many members do not have the resources to create their own transaction network. Most processors are also large acquirers and some even issuers.

Examples of Processors are:

- **Global Payment Systems**
- **First Data Resources (FDR)**
- **Vital**

ISO/MSP

An independent sales organization or member service provider is a non-association organization that performs merchant solicitation, sales or services on behalf of a member bank.

Many Acquirers are actually properly labeled as ISOs, and those without a member bank partner, are not association members. These larger Acquirer/ISOs are commonly referred to a "Super ISOs" while the smaller companies perform mostly sales and support roles are considered their "Sub-ISOs."

Merchant

A merchant is an Acquirer or ISO's customer or any business that sells goods or services and accepts Visa or MasterCard as payment.

Bankcard Fees

The components of bankcard fees are:

- **Interchange/Assessments**
- **Authorization Fees**
- **Processing Fees**
- **Processor Optional Fees**
- **Chargeback and Retrieval Fees**
- **T & E Authorization and Processing Fees**
- **Ancillary Communication and Network Fees**
- **Hardware and Software Fees**

Interchange

Visa and MasterCard are at the center of the transaction process, maintaining the flow of funds between issuers and acquirers. During Interchange, fees are deducted by the issuer from the transaction amount and the issuer pays the net amount to the acquirer. These are called interchange fees. Interchange is often used to refer to the amount the Acquirers pay the Issuers for each transaction and is determined on a transaction-by-transaction basis depending on many factors including; risk, merchant type and method of payment.

Clearing refers to the exchange of financial information. Settlement refers to the exchange of the actual funds for the transaction and the associated fees.

Clearing and Settlement occur simultaneously. The acquirer credits the merchant's deposit account for the dollar amount of the sale (less the merchant discount fee). The acquirer sends the transaction to a processor, who transports it through a data network, to INET (for MasterCard transactions) or VisaNet (for Visa transactions). (Note, some acquirers are also processors)

Visa and MasterCard transmit the transaction to the issuer, credit the acquirer and debits the issuer for the amount of the transaction. The Acquirer/Processor then funds the merchant for the sale, again less the discount fee.

In essence, the issuer pays the acquirer for the transaction via the Visa and MasterCard Interchange system. Interchange makes it possible for the issuing banks and acquiring banks to exchange information, transactions and money on a standardized basis.

Visa and MasterCard each own and operate their own international processing system. These systems connect thousands of banks around the world. Member Institutions use these networks to transmit information about bankcard transactions.

Visa & MasterCard

To Summarize:

Visa and MasterCard are independent, competing card associations comprised of over 20,000 member banks.

The Card Associations offer products on both the cardholder issuing and merchant acquiring side of the business to facilitate a complete system of electronic currency.

Cards are issued to consumers with credit spending limits, revolving interest rates and fees.

Merchants are enrolled to accept and deposit credit card sales through member acquiring banks.

The Associations role is primarily branding and marketing, governing and enforcing Issuing to acquiring rules and regulations, and managing and settling interchange.

A member bank may be both a card issuing and merchant acquiring institution.

The Card Associations have rules and regulations governing how industry risk is handled.

Merchant interchange fees are paid from the Acquirer bank to the Issuer.

Issuing banks market a variety of card products including: Classic, Gold or Platinum cards; commercial, business, corporate, fleet, or purchasing cards; and check cards.

Interchange fees vary depending on the type of card product and how it is accepted.

► **Chapter Five** ◄

The Anatomy of a Credit Card

ANSI Standard X4.13-1983 is the system used by most national credit-card systems.

What the Numbers Mean

Illustration by Rosaleah Rautert

The front of your credit card has a lot of numbers -- here's an example of what they might mean.

Here is what some of the numbers stand for:

The first digit in your credit-card number signifies the system:

3 - Travel/Entertainment cards (such as American Express and Diners Club)
4 - Visa
5 - MasterCard
6 - Discover Card

The **structure** of the card number varies by system. For example, American Express card numbers start with 37; Carte Blanche and Diners Club with 38.

50

©Performance Training Systems

American Express - Digits three and four are type and currency, digits five through 11 are the account number, digits 12 through 14 are the card number within the account, and digit 15 is a check digit.

Visa - Digits two through six are the bank number, digits seven through 12 or seven through 15 are the account number, and digit 13 or 16 is a check digit.

MasterCard - Digits two and three, two through four, two through five or two through six are the bank number (depending on whether digit two is a 1, 2, 3 or other). The digits after the bank number up through digit 15 are the account number, and digit 16 is a check digit.

Now that we know what the numbers stand for, let's examine the stripe on the back.

The Stripe

The stripe on the back of a credit card is a **magnetic stripe**, often called a **magstripe**. The magstripe is made up of tiny iron-based magnetic particles in a plastic-like film. Each particle is really a tiny **bar magnet** about 20-millionths of an inch long.

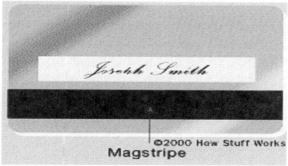

Illustration by Rosaleah Rautert
Your card has a magstripe on the back and a place for the signature.

©Performance Training Systems

A magstripe reader as found in electronic data capture (EDC) terminals, registers and numerous other electronic devices can understand the information on magstripe. If a terminal won't accept your card, the stripe may be dirty or scratched.

An erased magstripe (The most common causes for erased magstripes are exposure to magnets, like the small ones used to hold notes and pictures on the refrigerator, and exposure to a store's electronic article surveillance (EAS) tag demagnetizer.)

Information on the Stripe

There are three tracks on the magstripe. Each track is about one-tenth of an inch wide. The ISO/IEC standard 7811, which is used by banks, specifies:

- **Track one is 210 bits per inch (bpi), and holds 79 6-bit plus parity bit read-only characters.**
- **Track two is 75 bpi, and holds 40 4-bit plus parity bit characters.**
- **Track three is 210 bpi, and holds 107 4-bit plus parity bit characters.**

Your credit card typically uses only tracks one and two. Track three is a read/write track (which includes an encrypted PIN, country code, currency units and amount authorized), but its usage is not standardized among banks.

The information on track one is contained in two formats: A, which is reserved for proprietary use of the card issuer; and B, which includes the following:

Start sentinel - one character
Format code="B" - one character (alpha only)
Primary account number - up to 19 characters
Separator - one character
Country code - three characters
Name - two to 26 characters
Separator - one character
Expiration date or separator - four characters or one character
Discretionary data - enough characters to fill out maximum record length (79 characters total)
End sentinel - one character
Longitudinal redundancy check (LRC) - one character
LRC is a form of computed check character.
The format for track two, developed by the banking industry, is as follows:
Start sentinel - one character
Primary account number - up to 19 characters
Separator - one character
Country code - three characters
Expiration date or separator - four characters or one character
Discretionary data - enough characters to fill out maximum record length (40 characters total)
LRC - one character

For more info on standards go to www.ansi.org

► Chapter Six ◄

The Transaction Flow

Here are the steps involved in a typical retail credit card transaction:

Step 1   The consumer purchases goods or services from the merchant.

Step 2   The merchant transmits the transaction to the acquirer, by sliding the card through the terminal or magnetic stripe reader. The most common device is a credit card processing terminal. If the device cannot read the card, the merchant will manually enter the card information and get a manual imprint of the credit card.

The terminal then transmits the sales authorization request via a standard phone line connection to the acquiring bank.

Step 3	The acquiring bank routes the transaction to a processor and then to the associations - Visa System (Visa Net) or MasterCard System (INET).
Step 4	The association system then routes the transaction to the issuing bank and requests an approval.
Step 5	The issuing bank sends back the response. If the cardholder is approved the issuing bank assigns and transmits the authorization code back to the association.
Step 6	The association then sends the authorization code back to the acquiring bank.
Step 7	The acquiring bank routes the approval code or response to the merchant terminal. The merchant terminal prints a receipt for the cardholder to sign, which obligates the cardholder to pay the amount approved.

Step 8   Issuer bills the consumer.

Step 9   Consumer pays the bill.

Settlement

Settlement is the actual transfer of funds to the appropriate parties. Generally, at the end of the day, the merchant will review all their sales, credits, voids and totals in their terminal. Once all transactions are verified they will settle, or close, their batch and transmit the information to the acquirer for deposit to their bank account. The acquiring bank routes the transaction through the appropriate settlement system against the appropriate card-issuing bank.

The card-issuing bank routes the transfer back through the settlement system for the amount of the sales draft, less the appropriate discount fee, to the acquiring bank's account. The acquiring bank then deposits the amount to the merchant's bank account. The merchant usually has their money within 48-72 hours.

There are several variations of this procedure on the front end depending on the program the merchant is utilizing.

For example a restaurant may want to be able to track servers to more easily settle tips at the end of the shift. A hotel or car rental agency may want to get a pre-approval before the customer checks in or uses the service. A bar may want to open a tab for its customers.

Each processor has pre-built programs that can requested based upon the merchant's type of business.

Internet Processing

Here are the steps involved in a typical Internet transaction. This is assuming the merchant has a shopping cart and payment gateway installed on their website.

Step 1   The cardholder selects goods or services from the merchant's website. As each item is selected it is placed in the customers shopping cart.

Step 2   The customer verifies the items to be purchased, selects the shipping method and any other delivery options. The checkout button is clicked and the order is totaled for the customer. If all is acceptable the customer clicks the appropriate selection i.e. Process Order, Buy Now, Order Now, Checkout.

Step 3   The customer is then transmitted to a secure payment gateway. This allows the customer to enter the credit card information in a safe mode.

Step 4   Once the information is entered, the gateway encrypts the data and transmits the transaction to the acquirer.

Step 5   The acquiring bank routes the transaction to the Visa System (Visa Net) or MasterCard System (INET) who then routes the transaction to the issuing bank and requests an approval. Issuing banks use AVS (Address Verification System) and/or CVV (Card Verification Value) to prevent fraudulent

---

©Performance Training Systems

	use of consumer's credit card information.
Step 6	The issuing bank sends back the response. If the cardholder is approved the issuing bank assigns and transmits the authorization code back to the acquirer bank.
Step 7	The acquirer bank processes the transaction and sends the authorization code back to the merchant's secure gateway.
Step 8	The gateway displays an approval number for the customer, which usually advises them to print out a receipt at that time.
Step 9	The gateway software will also email a receipt to the customer at this time and an order notification to the merchant for processing and shipment.
Step 10	The merchant ships the merchandise to the customer.
Step 11	Usually at a specified time the payment gateway will automatically process the batch for the day.
Step 12	The acquirer/processor routes the transaction through the appropriate settlement system against the appropriate card-issuing bank.

Step 13   The card-issuing bank routes the transfer back through the appropriate settlement system for the amount of the sales draft, less the appropriate discount fee, to the acquiring bank's account.

Step 14   The acquirer then deposits the funds into the merchant's bank account. The merchant usually has their money within 48-72 hours.

Step 15   The cardholder's bank bills the cardholder for the amount of the purchase.

Step 16   Consumer pays the bill.

Just remember, a payment gateway serves the same function as a credit card terminal. There are multiple payment gateways on the market. Many have sophisticated fraud prevention tools and can assist the merchant in controlling chargebacks.

Payment gateways also provide what is commonly called a virtual terminal along with a shopping cart. The virtual terminal allows the merchant to process manual credit card transactions from location where there is an Internet connection.

For instance, a merchant may have a website taking orders 24 hours a day. And he may also travel to trade shows twice a month. If he has Internet access at the trade show, or at his hotel, he can process manual orders from his virtual terminal, which is web-based.

Internet transactions use several encryption technologies including Secure Socket Layer (SSL) protocol. For more information on encryption technologies and SSL go to:

http://developer.netscape.com/docs/manuals/security/sslin/contents.htm

► Chapter Seven ◄

Interchange

Every time a cardholder uses a credit card, the merchant is charged a percentage of each transaction, usually called a discount fee. The discount rate is largely comprised of the interchange and assessments. Interchange is the price charged by the issuing bank directly to the acquirer for processing the transaction. Profit comes from selling above this cost - the discount rate.

All other cards such as American Express, Diners, JCB and Discover set their own discount rates.

There are so many different categories and interchange rates, most Acquirers give their agents and ISOs give a blended buy-rate.

Generally, the discount fee that a merchant is charged depends on several factors including:

- **Interchange Category (Type of Business)**
- **Card Present/Card Not Present**
- **Retail or Internet**
- **Merchant Credit Standing**
- **Risk Potential**

A retail business will naturally be charged a lower rate than a mail order business due to the fact that the chance for fraud is much less with a card present transaction.

The normal terms for these fee categories are as follows:

Qualified Rate – the lowest rate a merchant will receive – this is when the merchant swipes the card and the credit card terminal reads it properly and the transaction is batched within the specified time frame.

Mid-Qualified – this is a rate that does not qualify for the lowest interchange level. This could be a hand keyed transaction or MOTO/internet merchant.

Non-Qualified – these are the highest rates. These are rates for purchasing cards, foreign cards or paper-based transactions.

There are over 32 different interchange levels. These terms mean different things depending on your acquirer. Always check with your ISO or acquiring bank for rate clarification.

► Chapter Eight ◄

Typical Merchant Fees

Lets review the most common fees that may be charged to merchants (in alphabetical order):

Address Verification Fee

The fee charged to the merchant to perform address verification.

Annual Fee

This is a yearly fee charged by ISO's and acquirers to maintain a merchant's account. This is also called a renewal fee, subscription fee, or annual membership fee.

Application Fee

This is the fee associated with processing an initial application from a new merchant. This covers the overhead costs of credit bureaus, phone verifications and data input.

Cancellation Fee

This is the fee charged by the ISO or acquirer if a merchant cancels his contract before the specified contract period expires.

Chargeback Fee

This is the fee charged by a bank when a chargeback is issued to a merchant. This varies from $15.00 – 30.00 per transaction. (Plus the actual amount of the chargeback sale)

Check Guarantee Fees

Check Guarantee fees are basically structured similar to credit card processing fees. There is usually a percentage rate, transaction fee, statement fee, monthly minimum and application fee.

Check Verification Fees

Check verification does not guarantee checks. Check verification checks whether the check writer has a history of writing bad checks. There is usually not a percentage fee associated with check verification.

Standard fees usually include a flat fee transaction fee, monthly minimum and/or statement fee.

Debit Fees

Debit fees vary based on the debit network that issues the debit card. Debit fees are comprised of network fees and transaction fees. Check with your ISO or acquirer for your exact debit fees.

The network will either charge a flat fee or a small percentage of the transaction. The acquirer may also have a debit card statement fee ranging from $3.00 - $10.00 per month.

Discount Fee (Per Transaction)

The discount rate is the fee charged by the acquirer to the merchant to process each transaction. This rate is dependent upon several factors, but usually the rate is either a retail (card present) merchant or a MOTO/Internet (card not present) merchant. (Refer to Chapter 7)

Retail Rates are lower because they present less risk than card not present transactions. Conversely card not present rates are higher due to the increased risk exposure to the bank.

For instance if the retail discount fee is 1.65% for a swiped transaction, then the merchant will be charged $1.65 for a $100.00 sale.

Rates with no transaction fee are called bundled rates. The cost of the transaction is built into the discount rate; bundled rates are usually used for merchants with a very small average ticket, like a dry cleaner, quick-serve or restaurant.

Also, if a retail merchant swipes a card and the magnetic strip cannot be read, an additional fee will apply because the card number will have to be manually entered. This is called a mid-qualified transaction or surcharge (these are high profit transactions.) These terms vary depending upon your bank. Always check with the Acquirer or ISO if there are rate fee questions.

If a merchant processes retail and Internet transactions the bank may require that they maintain two merchant accounts for each type of transaction.

Equipment Warranty Plan

This is a monthly or annual fee that will replace or repair a merchant's terminal if it malfunctions or breaks.

Internet Payment Gateway Fees

A monthly fee associated with maintaining a merchant's secure payment gateway.

Payment gateways also vary. Usually there is a setup fee, a monthly gateway fee, and/or a transaction fee.

The monthly gateway is usually between $10.00-$25.00, and the transaction fee ranges from .05 - .15 per sale.

Investigation Fee

This fee is charged by some banks to investigate or research merchant transactions.

Monthly Statement Fee

This is the monthly fee charged to the merchant in order to produce a monthly accounting of all transactions. This will usually breakdown their total sales by day, average ticket amount and total charges.

Monthly Minimum Fee

This is a set minimum the bank wants to earn from each account. Monthly minimum fees range from $10.00 - $25.00. That means if the merchant doesn't process any transactions, the bank will still receive the monthly minimum fee income in order to service the account.

Let's look at a merchant with a monthly minimum of $25.00. If they processed $1,000.00 in charges and the discount rate is 1.65%, the monthly discount fees will be $16.50 – they did not reach the $25.00 minimum, so they will be charged the difference of $8.50.

If they ran $10,000 in sales at a 1.65% discount rate, the monthly discount fee would be $165.00, so they would not be charged the $25.00 monthly minimum fee.

The monthly minimum only comes into play for low sales volume merchants.

Retrieval Fee

Fee charged to process a retrieval request.

Transaction Fee

This is a fee charged to the merchant to authorize a transaction. This fee for retail is usually .20 - .25 per sale and for MOTO it ranges between .28 - .35 per sale. In a bundled discount fee the transaction fees are included in the discount rate.

Voice Authorization Fee

This is the fee charged if the merchant calls to Visa/MasterCard for a manual voice authorization.

Wireless Fees

Wireless terminals require a wireless network to process transactions. The monthly wireless access fees range from $15.00 – $30.00 and additional per transaction fees can range from .05-.35 per transaction depending on the carrier. Often, a wireless setup fee is required that can range from $50.00 - $99.00.

▶ Chapter Nine ◀

Credit Card Disputes

Disputes

No system or industry is perfect, and in one with so many transactions and potential for user error, mistakes, and sometimes fraud occurs. To protect the payment system, consumers, and merchants from abuse and excessive costs, there are remedies to handle disputes between members.

The basics of this process are in the retrieval request and the chargeback. Requesting of information (particularly sales drafts) to clarify a sale is called the retrieval request and the reversing of unauthorized or incorrect sales is a chargeback.

Retrievals

There is often a need for clarification before a transaction is considered for dispute. If the cardholder simply doesn't recognize the merchant's name on the credit card bill they may request a copy of the sales receipt bearing their signature.

To comply with these requests, merchants must print receipts from their terminals (an electronic card reading device) or imprint the card with a slide over a pre-printed carbon form.

Retrieval Functions

- Storage of paper (hardcopy) sales drafts and film cartridges

- Retrieval of items in the hardcopy retrieval and chargeback process

- Request Fulfillment

Sales Draft Storage

In addition to properly obtaining signed receipts the merchant or the acquirer must save the sales receipts (also called drafts). Acquirers or merchants are required to hold drafts for a total of 10 years, of which 3 years must be held on-site. Both merchants and acquirers store hardcopy sales drafts or POS tape.

Sales Draft Retrieval

Acquirers receive requests from issuing banks. Visa and MasterCard regulations stipulate that a request must be fulfilled within 30 days from the date of receipt. Any request not fulfilled within that time frame can be charged back to the merchant.

Request Fulfillment

Requests for all hardcopy sales drafts are fulfilled as quickly as possible for disbursement to the issuing bank. MasterCard requires that all retrieval requests be fulfilled electronically through the MasterCom electronic image processing system.

Visa will allow requests to be fulfilled through the mail and via Visa's Copy Request Manager System.

Chargebacks and Collections

When an issuer disputes a transaction (either at the request of the cardholder or for reasons of their own), the matter is resolved, a chargeback, or a compliance case. In a chargeback, the issuer returns the transaction to the acquirer.

Chargebacks result either from cardholder disputes or from rules violations by the merchant or acquirer; they help enforce operating rules and correct transaction errors.

The initial, or first, chargeback is initiated by the issuer. It can result from the issuer finding an error in the transaction, or it may result from a cardholder complaint. Visa and MasterCard have developed standard procedures and time frames for submitting and processing chargebacks.

The Chargeback Process

The chargeback process begins when an issuer, on its own behalf or in defense of a cardholder, returns a transaction previously submitted by the Acquirer. Presentment is the stage of interchange when the acquirer, via the Visa and MasterCard system, presents the issuer with the transaction information. The issuer is automatically charged for the transaction during settlement, which takes place at the same time as clearing.

In other words, the issuer receives information about a transaction, for which it has already paid, and realizes that the transaction may be invalid.

At this point, if sufficient evidence of fraud or error is provided by the cardholder and is substantiated, the issuer may charge the transaction back to the acquirer.

Functions of the Acquirers

- Determine legitimacy of chargebacks presented by issuers, try to substantiate all "representable" items on behalf of their merchants
- Handle arbitration of chargebacks if the representment is disputed by the issuer
- Handle collection of amounts from the merchants
- Acceptance of incoming collections cases from Issuers
- Acceptance of outgoing collection cases from merchants
- Submit Arbitration/Compliance issues to Card Associations
- Reversal of inaccurate merchant transactions

► Chapter Ten ◄

Debit and Check Card Processing

- In 2002 Visa check and debit MasterCard check cards accounted for 8.16 billion signature-based transactions.

- Signature-based purchases totaled $317.7 billion.

- Three quarters of all adult bank account holders in the U.S. had an ATM/debit card.

- Online debit (pin-based) accounted for 10% of electronic transactions in 2001.

- Offline debit (check card transaction) accounted for 18% of electronic transactions in 2001.

- Of the 78.6 billion total noncash payments, signature-based, or offline debit cards accounted for 5.3 billion (6.7%) while PIN-based debit cards accounted for 3 billion (3.8%) in 2001.

- 87% of ATM/debit cardholders use the card to make purchases at the point-of-sale.

- Debit card use increases about 25% every year.

- It is estimated that debit will be the most popular form of non-cash payment by 2008.

Source: ATM & Debit News, Retail Payments Research Project, Card Forum

Debit is the fastest growing form of payment. A debit card accesses the cardholder's bank account to secure and hold the authorization amount against available funds.

There are two types of debit transactions:

- **Online (PIN Based) – ATM Like**
- **Offline (Signature Based) – Check Card**

A regular debit or ATM card (without the Visa or MasterCard logo) may only be used through the debit networks.

This means that the debit card will work at any ATM machine but in order to be accepted at a merchant business, the merchant must have the debit service activated and a pin pad attached to the credit card terminal.

A check card (Visa or MasterCard logo) can access all the debit/ATM networks and has the ability to run through the credit card networks like a credit card transaction.

Rates for online debit are usually just a small transaction fee. Pricing for check cards is similar to a credit card transaction, which has a percentage and transaction fee.

For example, compare the fees on a $1,000.00 sale for a merchant with a 1.65% rate and a .25 transaction fee for credit card transactions.

Online	**Offline**
(Requires Pin Pad)	**(Check Card, No Pin)**
Usually flat rate approx .40	**1.65% +. 25**
Total cost = .40	Total cost = 16.75

By running the sale as an online debit the merchant would save $16.35 for a single transaction.

The potential savings to merchants with higher ticket sales is tremendous. Today there are roughly 823,000 POS terminals equipped with the pin pads. With an estimated number of 5 million POS terminals installed that leaves over 4 million potential customers.

Some of the most popular debit networks are:

- **Accel**
- **Cash Station**
- **Cirrus**
- **Explorer**
- **Honor East**
- **Honor West (BankMate)**
- **Interlink**
- **MAC**
- **Maestro**
- **Magic Line**
- **NYCE**
- **Pulse**
- **Shazam**

▶ Chapter Eleven ◀

Electronic Benefits Transfer (EBT)

EBT programs allow participants to receive and access their government paid benefits electronically using a magstripe card and to redeem their benefits for cash assistance or food stamp programs.

What are the benefits of EBT?

- EBT offers a more cost-efficient and secure benefit delivery system.
- Recipients no longer have to go to banks or check cashing agents to receive their cash or food stamp benefits.
- Recipients no longer need to carry large amount of cash or food stamps. They can withdraw their benefits as needed.
- Recipients are no longer stigmatized by using food coupons since EBT makes shoppers with food stamp benefits look like any other shoppers.
- If the EBT Access Card is lost or stolen, it cannot be used without the PIN. The card is easily canceled and replaced.
- EBT eliminates the labor-intensive process of storage, delivery and accounting for the paper coupons at the federal and state levels.
- Retailers are able to provide better customer service in the checkout lane because EBT transactions are faster and more efficient than paper coupons.
- Retailers no longer have to count, bundle and deposit paper food coupons at their bank because the EBT settlement process is automatic and provides a payment to the retailer's account within two business days.

- All of the food stamp dollars are spent on food because change is never given.
- EBT creates an electronic record of transactions, making it easier to identify and document instances of fraudulent activity.

EBT is not a big money maker for our industry but is required if selling into niche markets like grocery or convenience retailers.

► Chapter Twelve ◄

Check Processing

- According to the Depository Financial Institution check study sponsored by the Federal Reserve in 2001, there are 49.6 Billion checks written annually in the U.S. for a total value of $47.7 trillion dollars.

- This was the first comprehensive study of U.S. check volume since 1979. Since 1979, the average value per check has risen from $757.00 to $961.00 per check.

- In 2001 there were over 300 million returned checks totaling $197 Billion dollars. The average value of each returned check is $656.00.

- Businesses are the heaviest writers and receivers of checks, accounting for 40% of the total value of check payments.

- Electronic Check (e-check) Volume Reaches 517.74 Million Transactions in 2002

- Total dollar volume of e-check transactions was $101.54 billion in 2002.

Source: Federal Reserve Check Study, Nacha

One of the major challenges small businesses face is check loss. If merchants don't accept checks, they lose significant revenue.

There are several check products that can be offered to help merchants control losses:

- **Check Guarantee** – This service will pay the merchant the full face value of the check if it is returned for insufficient funds. The check guarantee company assumes all risk for the check.

- **Check Verification** – This service will check your customer's information against a bad check writer's database and send back an approval or decline. The merchant assumes responsibility for collecting the check. (Many verification companies offer check collection programs)

- **Check Conversion or Electronic Check Conversion (ECC)** – This service allows the check to be converted into an electronic transaction and deposited into the merchant's bank account. It is similar to a credit card transaction. Depending on the service provider, the check can be guaranteed, verified and/or imaged.

- **RCK (Represented Check) Service** – This service converts a returned paper check to an electronic check and represents the check for payment through the Automated Clearing House (ACH) system.

Check guarantee and verification processing are similar to credit card processing. The check is either hand entered or entered through a check reader, which transmits the check data to the approval center. The check company then authorizes or declines the check based on the information in the database. The transaction takes approximately as long as a credit card transaction.

Electronic Check Conversion

Merchants using this process accept customer checks, swipe them through a reader converting the check to an electronic funds transfer (EFT), stamp the check "ACH Processed," and hand it back to the customer.

It basically takes a paper check and turns it into an electronic transaction similar to a credit card transaction.

The advantages of check conversion are:

- **Fast Funding To Merchants**
- **Reduces Check Losses**
- **Enhanced Reporting**
- **Lower Overhead (no more trips to the bank)**

Go to this visa site to review their POS check service presentation:

www.usa.visa.com/business/merchants/pos_check_service.html

Redeposit or Represent Check (RCK)

This service improves the merchant's collections efforts and reduces paper. The merchant can purchase an in-house system or contract with an outside company to automatically forward all returned checks for immediate RCK collection. The paper check is converted to an electronic transaction, which receives priority clearing at the customer's bank.

The merchant can process checks and resubmit checks on any given day, increasing collection rates on bad checks by timing the transaction with the check writer's pay schedule.

Check Imaging

Check imaging is the ability for the merchant to take an image or picture of the check at the point-of-sale.

Today's check readers provide magnetic ink character recognition (MICR) reading accuracy in the 99%+ range. Imaging is useful when customer contact information is required in the event of a check written either fraudulently or non-sufficient funds (NSF).

In the event of a NSF check, a normal check conversion program will represent the check automatically. It is not until the maximum number of retries is completed that the merchant or check collection company actually sees the check.

For more information on electronic check processing go to:

Electronic Check Council – http://ecc.nacha.org

The mission of the council is to design, propose and monitor pilots for electronic payment services that enable the conversion of paper checks to electronic entries conveniently, reliably, securely and on a cost effective basis; to provide information on check conversion, legal and regulatory issues, and electronic services to the NACHA family; and to provide a forum for the resolution of electronic check issues.

▶ Chapter Thirteen ◀
ACH Processing

- ACH (Automated Clearing House) payments have increased over 500 percent since 1979. The Federal Reserve study noted that ACH, processing is poised for meaningful growth.

- The number of ACH payments originated by financial institutions increased to 8.05 billion in 2002, up 13.6 percent from 2001. These payments were valued at $21.7 trillion. Including payments originated by the Federal government, there were a total of 8.94 billion ACH payments in 2002 worth more than $24.4 trillion.

- Over 115 million consumers and over 4 million businesses utilize the ACH Network.

- In 2001, 18% of all ACH transactions represented business to business payments, 78% business to consumer or vice versa, and 3% were new ACH products such as check conversion, e-checks and re-presented checks.

- It is projected that by 2006 ACH transaction will exceed 15 billion.

- More than 200 million e-checks were processed in 2001. E-checks debit the consumers bank account to pay for goods or services through the ACH network.

- In 2001 there were 88.7 million e-checks processed at the POS, 74.6 million originated from the Internet, and 8.7 million originated from the telephone.

- The National Automated Clearinghouse Association (NACHA) stats show that 25.99 million re-presented check entries were processed in 2002.

Source: Federal Reserve Check Study, NACHA

An ACH transaction simply allows the merchant to charge a customer utilizing the ACH network by deducting funds directly from the customer's bank account.

ACH processing is being used for many purposes including: Direct Payroll/Bank Deposits, Recurring Payments (monthly ongoing payments), Online Payments, Telephone Payment, Check Collection, E-check purchases, and business to business payments.

Great potential customers for ACH check services are:

- **Cable Companies**
- **Cell Phone Companies**
- **Child Care Facilities**
- **Churches**
- **Collection Agencies**
- **Diaper Services**
- **Doctors**
- **Furniture Rental Stores**
- **Government Agencies**
- **Health Clubs**
- **Home Security Companies**
- **Hospitals**
- **Insurance Companies**
- **Internet Service Providers**
- **Janitorial Companies**
- **Karate Studios**
- **Lawn Care Services**

- Leasing Companies
- Mail Order
- Multi-Level Marketing (MLM)
- Musical Instrument Rentals
- Newspapers
- Non-Profits
- Orthodontists
- Pager Services
- Pest Control
- Property Management
- Tanning Salons
- Telemarketing Companies
- Uniform Rental
- Utility Companies

For more information on ACH processing go to: www.nacha.org

NACHA is a not-for-profit trade association that develops operating rules and business practices for the Automated Clearing House (ACH) Network and for other areas of electronic payments.

NACHA activities and initiatives facilitate the adoption of electronic payments in the areas of Internet commerce, electronic bill payment and presentment (EBPP), financial electronic data interchange (EDI), international payments, electronic checks, electronic benefits transfer (EBT) and student lending.

NACHA promotes the use of electronic payment products and services, such as Direct Deposit and Direct Payment. NACHA represents more than 12,000 financial institutions through our network of regional ACH associations and has over 600 members in seven industry councils and corporate affiliate membership program.

► Chapter Fourteen ◄

Gift Cards

- Bain & Co. a leading research firm predicted gift card sales would reach $38 billion in 2002, up from $13 billion in 1998.

- 88% of all major retailers sell gift cards.

- 80% of Americans have heard of a gift card.

- 45% of the U.S. population has used a gift card.

- It is estimated that there are over 1 billion gift cards currently issued.

Source: Thompson Financial, Greensheet

Major companies like Starbucks and Home Depot have popularized the use of gift cards. They provide many benefits for merchants:

- **Increased store traffic**
- **Increased sales**
- **Increased brand identity and loyalty**
- **Increased profits by breakage, which are unspent gift card balances**
- **Reduced employee fraud**
- **Reduced employee overhead and administration**
- **Increased customer service to customers (fast checkouts and enhanced record keeping)**
- **Improved reporting capability**

Gift cards are swiped through the credit card terminal and activated. The amount of the card is either pre-determined or loaded when activated. The merchant increases cash flow because the gift card will most likely not be redeemed for some time.

The customer keeps the card in their purse or wallet; the merchant builds brand identity and advertising every time they open their purse or wallet. The customer returns and presents the gift card for purchase; any leftover money is still stored on the card.

The customer keeps the card and by later returning to the store, increases the merchant's store traffic and gives the merchant another opportunity to make additional sales. If the customer never returns the unused amount on the card it is called "Breakage". Breakage provides another profit center for the merchant.

A recent study indicated that 86% of customers use 100% of the card value. The remaining 14% is never redeemed, leaving the merchant an excellent profit.

► Chapter Fifteen ◄

Loyalty Cards

According to a recent article by Colloquy Magazine *"A loyalty program is one that seeks to identify, maintain and increase the yield from customers through long-term, interactive, value-added relationships."*

In this competitive business climate, many merchants are looking for more innovative ways to increase customer loyalty. This is one of the hottest segments of the merchant services industry. There are thousands of loyalty programs in the marketplace. The loyalty industry is estimated at $5 billion and rising.

Everywhere companies are implementing and advertising customer loyalty programs. Loyalty programs are now available at your local carwash, auto repair, video store, retailer and restaurant.

Companies realize that their most precious asset is their existing customer base. Merchants are acutely aware that it costs much more to acquire a new customer than to market to an existing customer. By utilizing a loyalty program merchants can gain a competitive advantage by analyzing demographic data and customer buying patterns.

Loyalty programs can be customized, but for the most part they award customers for shopping based upon number of visits or dollars spent. For instance, a company may want to offer a 20% discount on a customer's 10th visit. Or give away a free movie rental on the 20th rental. The potential is unlimited.

Loyalty programs offer many advantages to merchants:

- **Increase advertising opportunities**
- **Increase sales**
- **Establish stronger relationships**
- **Increase customer retention**
- **Increase customer base from referrals and added benefits**
- **Increase reporting features**
- **Data mining of customer shopping and purchasing patterns**

Many of the new cards will be hybrid cards or multi-application cards. This means they may provide both gift and loyalty capabilities on a single card.

Loyalty applications are another excellent way to get your foot in the door of a potential customer. Merchants are much more willing to talk to someone about an opportunity to increase their traffic, profit and customer retention, than saving money on credit card processing.

Want more information on the loyalty industry? Visit www.colloquy.com/default.asp

▶ Chapter Sixteen ◀

Smart Cards

The **"smart"** credit card is an innovative application that involves all aspects of cryptography (secret codes). A smart card has a microprocessor built into the card itself.

Cryptography is essential to the functioning of these cards in several ways:

The user must verify identity each time a transaction is made, in much the same way that a PIN is used with an ATM.

The card and the card reader execute a sequence of encrypted sign/counter sign-like exchanges to verify that each is dealing with a legitimate counterpart.

Once established, the transaction itself is carried out in encrypted form to prevent anyone, including the cardholder or the merchant whose card reader is involved, from "eavesdropping" on the exchange and later impersonating either party to defraud the system.

This elaborate protocol is conducted in such a way that it is invisible to the user, except for the necessity of entering a PIN to begin the transaction.

Smart cards first saw general use in France in 1984. They are now hot commodities that are expected to someday replace the simple plastic cards most of people use now at least in Europe. American Express, Visa and MasterCard are leading the way in the United States with their smart card technologies.

The chips in these cards are capable of many kinds of transactions. For example, a purchase could be made from a credit card account, debit card account or from a stored value account that's reloadable. The enhanced memory and processing capacity of the smart card is many times that of traditional magnetic-stripe cards and can accommodate several different applications on a single card. It can also hold identification information, keep track of participation in an affinity (loyalty) program or provide access to a customer's office.

Potential advantages would be to eliminate the need to shuffle through cards to find the right one - the smart card will be the only one needed!

Experts say that internationally accepted smart cards will be increasingly available over the next several years. Many parts of the world already use them, but their reach is limited. The smart card will eventually be available to anyone who wants one, but for now, it's only available to those participating in special programs.

Magnetic stripe technology remains in wide use in the U.S. However, the data on the stripe can easily be read, written, deleted or changed with off-the-shelf equipment. Therefore, the stripe is really not the best place to store sensitive information. To protect the consumer, businesses in the U.S. have invested in extensive online mainframe-based computer networks for verification and processing.

In Europe, such an infrastructure did not develop and instead the card carries the intelligence. There are advantages and disadvantages to both systems.

The microprocessor on the smart card is there for security. The host computer and card reader actually "talk" to the microprocessor. The microprocessor enforces access to the data on the card.

The most common smart card applications are:

- Credit Cards
- Electronic Cash
- Computer Security Systems
- Wireless Communication
- Loyalty Systems
- Prepaid Products
- Banking Applications
- Medical Record Management
- Government Identification

Additionally, smart cards can be used with a smart card reader attachment to a personal computer to authenticate a user.

Web browsers can also use smart card technology to supplement Secure Socket Layer (SSL) for improved security of Internet transactions.

The Opportunities in Smart Cards

Why have smart cards been slow to enter the U.S. market? According to the Tower Group "Converting U.S. payment cards alone from magnetic stripe to smart chip will cost $13.4 billion, with the merchant bearing $7.2 billion of the cost." Another reason is just common sense – the current magstripe based system works.

Although slow to take hold the are now being adopted at a rapid pace, with organizations like Target, the Postal Service and the U.S. Government leading the way.

Just be aware of the changes taking place and be ready to capitalize on them. The wide adoption of smart cards, it will help spur the replacement of obsolete processing equipment and provide Acquirers and ISOs new merchant sales opportunities.

► Chapter Seventeen ◄

Custom Card Applications

The development of custom applications for prepaid and smart cards is on the rise. The application for custom systems is basically unlimited. Here are some promising areas where applications have been or are being developed:

- **Payroll Cards**
- **Prepaid Products**
- **Online Insurance Benefits Verification**
- **Online Claims Processing**
- **Pharmacy Cards**
- **Insurance Card Programs**
- **ID Programs**
- **Mass Transit**
- **Parking Systems**
- **Child Support Payments**
- **College Campus Card Programs**
- **Time and Attendance Monitoring**
- **Travel Cards**
- **Corporate Incentive Cards**

Custom applications are a great way to enter a niche market. Keep your eyes open for new programs. New programs to merchants mean the potential for new equipment sales and more residuals.

©Performance Training Systems

► Chapter Eighteen ◄

Wireless Processing

Wireless processing allows a merchant to process transactions through a mobile POS terminal without the need for a dial-up phone line or electrical power. A wireless transaction utilizes a wireless network just like cell phones.

There are three main wireless networks in the United States:

- **CDPD (Cellular Digital Packet Data) – this technology is becoming obsolete**

- **Motient – owned and operated by Motient Corporation**

- **Mobitex – owned and operated by Cingular Interactive in the U.S.**

Each service provider has certain coverage areas, make sure to check the merchant's needs against the coverage area of each network.

Many acquirers use data network carriers such as U.S. Wireless Data. These service providers connect processors with the POS terminals. They route the transactions for merchants that do not have direct agreements with wireless network carriers.

They also offer value-added services such as report generation, activation and help desk support.

Advantages of Wireless

- Merchants who previously couldn't accept credit cards, now can
- Merchants pay lower discount rates due to swipe
- Increased merchant flexibility
- No power needed (good for trade shows, taxi drivers, sidewalk sale)
- Merchants can easily expand checkout lanes and remote promotional sales
- No phone lines required or phone line installation cost
- Faster transaction times – always on connection
- Reduced risk of taking a bad card
- Secure transactions
- Store and forward capability allows merchants to accept cards while out of their wireless coverage area

Great Markets for Wireless are:

- Delivery & Distribution Companies
- Plumbers & Electricians
- Towing & Locksmiths
- Heating & Air Conditioning
- Messenger Services
- Taxi & Limousine Companies
- Pizza Delivery
- Tool Trucks
- Window & Door Installation
- Car Detailing
- Carpenters & Home Maintenance
- Furniture Delivery
- Lawn & Pool Services
- Merchants That Value Flexibility or Speed

©Performance Training Systems

- Bike Rentals
- Stadiums & Arenas
- Amusement Parks
- Concert Pavilions
- Park & Recreation Centers
- Farmers Markets
- Flea Markets
- Marinas
- Golf Courses
- Colleges & Universities
- Raceways

▶ Chapter Nineteen ◀

MCommerce

- MCommerce (Mobile Commerce) refers to transacting business on mobile devices (cell phones and PDA's). This service is taking off overseas, especially in Japan. NTT DoCoMo's imode service has attracted 13 million users in just 11 months in Japan.

- Goldman Sachs estimates that the number of U.S. mobile wireless subscribers will increase from 86 million in 1999 to 232 million by 2005, a compounded annual growth rate of 28%. The growth of wireless Internet subscribers will increase from 3.5 million in 2000 to 151 million by 2005.

- The value of mobile data services is forecasted to reach nearly $45 billion by 2005 in the U.S. alone.

According to a MasterCard International white paper, there are three key enabling factors that will help bring mobile data services to the mass consumer market over the next few years.

- **Increased Internet enabled devices**
- **Improved mobile data download times**
- **Increase in mobile applications development**

Examples of mobile applications and uses include e-bills, retailing, ticketing, auctions, reservations, advertising, dynamic information management, loyalty programs and medical records.

Applications in use today involve alert-based services such as stock quotes, financial news, appointment notifications and offers of special discounts for tickets.

There are now programs that turn a PDA or cell phone into a mobile credit card machine. All that is needed is a magstripe reader and software package and merchants can utilize their wireless PDA or cell phone to process credit cards.

This will be a major market in the future.

▶ Chapter Twenty ◀

eCommerce

- There are over 385 million people with Internet access

- The average user logs on the Internet 19 times per month

- The average user spends over 10 hours per month viewing web pages

Source: neilson-netratings

ECommerce (Electronic Commerce) is the buying of goods and services via the Internet. The functions of an ecommerce web site include the presence of an online store, a method of payment processing, shipping/order fulfillment, customer service and promotion.

The basic components of an ecommerce site are:

- **Website Pages**
- **Shopping Cart**
- **Payment Processing Gateway**
- **Order Fulfillment System**
- **Hosting Solution**

What are the benefits of ecommerce?

    1. Convenience, ecommerce sites operate 24 hours a day 7 days a week. Lower Internal Costs.

    2. Internet commerce allows firms to eliminate the middleman in buyer-supplier transactions. Firms interact with

customers through e-mail rather than direct mail and direct sales associates. Information is distributed online instead of through costly catalogs.

3. Cheaper Processing Costs. Electronic payments are less expensive than live assisted calls.

4. Increased Speed of the Selling Process. Ecommerce companies receive revenue faster than traditional retail sellers.

5. Reduced Errors. The automated process tends to produce fewer errors than the traditional selling process.

6. Unlimited Shelf Space. Ecommerce companies can display/shelve an unlimited number/amount of goods.

7. Increased Global Presence. People from all over the world can access Ecommerce companies.

Ecommerce is on the rise according to an article written in April 2003, by Ryan Naraine in USA today. He states the e-commerce sector, once the face of the protracted dot-com slump, has emerged as a rare bright spot on the Internet with research firms predicting a banner year in 2003.

Despite a continued sluggish economy, business research firm eMarketer is predicting the total business-to-consumer (B2C) commerce market will reach $90.1 billion in 2003, a whopping $30 billion over 2002.

By 2005, the B2C e-commerce market is projected to reach $133 billion, eMarketer said. The statistics mirror projections from Jupiter Research that the market this year will reach $85.7 billion and $132.2 billion by 2005.

Excluding travel, eMarketer is projecting $58.2 billion in B2C retail revenue in 2003. Similarly, Jupiter Research statistics show non-travel e-commerce revenue will be in the range of $51.7 billion. Both firms indicate that more than half of the Web population has embraced online shopping.

The expected boom this year follows a retreat in 2001 when the first three quarters remained flat.

"After the traditional first quarter dip following the holiday season, online sales in the second quarter rose about $1.5 billion from first quarter of 2002 and kept growing from there, culminating in an all-time high of $14.3 billion," eMarketer said.

All told, last year was nice to the e-commerce sector. Statistics from the Department of Commerce showed spending reached $45.5 billion, a $10 billion increase over the previous year.

The good news is in stark contrast to a few years ago when e-commerce plays were going out of business at a rapid pace. Since then, success stories have emerged among the major plays such as Amazon.com, eBay, Barnes & Noble.com and airline ticketing clearinghouse Orbitz.

Even more encouraging, Jupiter Research reported, was that higher percentages of Web surfers have become more comfortable with the concept of online shopping.

Driven by online population growth, increased spending by buyers, and higher percentages of online shoppers (142 million consumers or 65 percent of the online population will have made a purchase online by 2007) Jupiter expects online retail spending to reach $105 billion by 2007, accounting for 5 percent of all U.S. retail spending and influencing 34 percent of all U.S. retail spending.

Jupiter found that the Internet affected $232 billion in offline spending in 2002 -- excluding automobiles, prescription drugs, financial services, and travel) -- and will grow to $573 billion by 2007.

Payment system consultants can penetrate this market by offering online payment gateways and virtual terminal products. There are several excellent products on the market, check with your ISO and acquirer to see which software your bank interfaces with.

For more Internet statistics go to:

www.internetstats.com/bus_list_cat.php3

http://ecommerce.internet.com

▶ Chapter Twenty One ◀
Processing Equipment

According to a recent article in ATM & Debit News in 2002 manufacturers shipped 1,956,731 terminals in the United States, an increase of 12.3% from the previous year.

Here are the approximate new terminal shipments in the U.S. by vendor for 2002:

Manufacturer	Units Shipped
Verifone	606,680
Hypercom	596,000
Ingenico	286,718
Lipman USA	160,000
MIST	70,000
Thales	42,000
Linkpoint	36,333
Schlumberger Sema	35,000

Source: ATM & Debit News

These numbers should give you a good idea about who holds what percentage of market share in the U.S. However, worldwide market share distribution is quite different.

Credit card processing equipment or point-of-sale devices (POS) gives the merchant the ability to electronically transmit transactions to their acquiring bank.

Optional POS systems may include software packages installed on a PC with a magnetic stripe reader, a cash register, a wireless unit, a kiosk, or custom developed system (usually for very large merchants).

For small to mid-size businesses, a standard credit card terminal and printer will do the job.

Terminals have drastically evolved over the years. The majority of terminals now are multi-application capable.

Multi-application capable means a terminal can process and support multiple services at the merchant countertop.

Current POS devices have the ability to process several types of applications:

- **Credit Card Transactions**
- **Gift/Loyalty Cards**
- **Prepaid Services (limited number)**
- **Check Processing**
- **Debit Transactions**
- **EBT**
- **Check Card Transactions**
- **Purchasing Cards**
- **Signature Capture**
- **Electronic Benefits Transfer**
- **Smart Cards**
- **Wireless**
- **Custom Applications**

There are multiple manufactures of POS terminals in the market place. The major manufactures of POS equipment are:

- **Hypercom**
- **Igenico**
- **Linkpoint**
- **Lipman USA**
- **Schlumberger**

- **Thales**
- **Verifone**

Future applications will include medical benefits verification, medical claims processing, government license renewals (i.e. fishing and hunting), many manufacturers already have applications for biometrics, age verification and many more.

Check with your ISO and acquirer to see what new products you will be able to offer in the future.

# Chapter Twenty Two

Leasing

Leasing is the ability to finance merchant equipment over time. Leasing allows the salesperson to offer the merchant an alternative to paying cash. A large number of the equipment sales in the bankcard industry are made utilizing lease financing.

When leasing equipment, the agent is paid a percentage of the payments the lessee (merchant) is going to make over the term of the lease. The lease company grades the lease, based on the merchant's credit, to determine the amount of funding or commission to the agent.

Gross funding amounts are based upon lease factors, which correspond to the term of the lease and customer credit rating. The lease company sets the factor assigned to each credit score.

Let's look at a $39.00 monthly lease payment for a term of 48 months with an "A" credit score with a lease factor of .0310.

To get the total funding amount divide $39.00 by .0310 for a total funding amount of $1258.06 – this is your gross funding amount. Remember you must deduct your equipment cost, doc fees if any, upfront payments not paid by merchant and any other overhead costs.

Usual lease terms are 12, 24, 36 and 48 months. Leasing is not renting - the merchant is committed to the contract for the term of the lease, it is non-cancelable. Most lease companies will let the merchant transfer the lease liability if the business is sold or let the merchant pay the lease off early.

In addition to the monthly lease payment the merchant will pay tax and a loss destruction waiver. The loss destruction waiver is small fee charged per month and serves as an insurance policy on the equipment. It's like buying a car, if you finance a car, insurance must be purchased. The merchant can avoid this fee by providing their own coverage with the lease company named as the loss payee.

At the end of the lease term the merchant will either return the equipment to the leasing company or purchase the equipment for fair market value. Fair market value is determined by the leasing company.

The advantages of leasing are as follows:

- **Requires very little upfront cash (usually 1 or 2 payments)**
- **Preserves existing capital, which can be used to start and maintain business**
- **Easily budgeted with a fixed lease payment**
- **100% tax deductible**
- **Older equipment can be upgraded to take advantage of newer technology**
- **Excellent selling tool to close more business**

Here are the normal steps to process a lease:

Step 1	Agent writes a contract between the merchant and lease company.
Step 2	Lease is faxed or sent to lease company for credit grading.
Step 3	Merchant is approved; equipment is downloaded and installed at merchant location.
Step 4	Original lease and required paperwork is sent to lease company for funding.
Step 5	Merchant verbally verifies the terms of the lease with the lease company.
Step 6	Lease company pays ISO funding amount based on credit score.
Step 7	Agent is paid commission.

Most lease companies currently are leasing only hardware, which means a physical piece of equipment. A few will lease software and payment gateways.

► Chapter Twenty Three ◄

Other Tier II Products

Here are several products you may want to lead with to create heightened interest or to bundle with your bankcard offering.

Electronic Receipt Capture (Terminal Specific)

Electronic Receipt Capture (ERC) creates a paperless system to manage customer receipts. By managing the storage of customer receipts, chargebacks to the merchant are greatly reduced. Many major retailers have already moved to ERC. Acquirers keep records of all receipts usually for a fee, and the merchant no longer has to worry about storage requirements or retrieving paper copies.

At checkout the customer's signature is captured electronically by a receipt capture device.

This is a great service for large volume merchants that have a hard time tracking retrieval and chargeback items.

Prepaid Phone Cards and Wireless (Terminal Specific)

The first electronic phone card was introduced in 1976. Now consumers can use phone cards to make calls within the U.S. and International markets at deeply discounted rates.

Phone cards are sold in dominations from $5.00 -$100.00 and are targeted to convenience users (i.e. travelers), EBT customers, gift givers, international customers, college students, truck drivers, and business travelers.

Phone cards can be reloaded through a credit card terminal, website or self-serve kiosk.

Prepaid wireless is a new and upcoming product. Vendors like AT&T and Verizon have entered the market. Customers can purchase prepaid minutes from retailers and activate their phone with a pin code. This is a great product for representatives selling into the grocery, convenience store and check cashing market.

Biometrics

- Total biometric revenues are expected to rise from $524 million in 2001 to $1.9 billion in 2005.

Biometrics has been used for years at government and high security facilities. It is now being introduced to the mass market.

Biometrics is a new tool merchants can utilize to combat fraud. It helps identify card users by their fingerprint, voice recognition, retina, or face scan.

This relatively new technology has made biometrics cost-effective and reliable. Now a person's true identity can be proved. Biometric proponents paint a world with no need for physical forms of identity like drivers licenses, passports or ID cards.

ATM Processing

Automated teller machines offer a great opportunity for upfront and residual income. ATMs are a great revenue generator for high traffic locations such as malls, gas stations and convenience stores. Not only do merchants earn money on every transaction conducted on their ATM, they sell more merchandise by giving consumers quick access to cash.

Many new ATMs have the ability to dispense pre-paid phones cards, coupons and even let consumer's access information via the Internet.

A merchant or a cash management service that he has procured, load the machine with cash. Consumers pay a surcharge to withdraw the cash and the merchant keeps a portion of the surcharge.

ATM Scrip Machine

This is an older form of an ATM machine. Scrip machines are a more affordable means for consumers to access cash. This is a solution for merchants not wanting to make a large investment in a full size ATM machine.

The consumers swipes their card through the scrip machine, after approval it will print a receipt, the consumers takes the receipt to the merchants counter and the merchant will physically give them their cash.

We are seeing a resurgence of the scrip machine. Many merchants prefer this option because they don't have to worry about restocking cash, theft and security. Additionally, many merchants, especially those in "closed-loop" environments, such as amusement parks, college campus' and malls, issue scrip that, instead of being redeemed for cash is instead useable only at their location, or with the closed loop. This is an excellent profit opportunity for the merchant.

©Performance Training Systems

Payroll Cards

This is a fairly new product making inroads with many employers. A payroll card allows employers to load a paycheck on to an employee debit card. The employee can now access pay through any ATM on the network the card was issued from. The employee is not required to have a bank account. This is a great product to target those segments of the population that have no bank account.

Payroll cards can be a standard debit card or Visa/Mastercard branded. Many companies are adding benefits to the card like insurance, long distance, rewards and travel.

For many employees they receive an instant raise due to high check cashing fees paid. It is estimated that roughly 15%-20% of Americans do not have a bank account.

Contactless Payments

Contactless payments are on the rise with programs like speedpass and paypass gaining popularity. Contactless payments can be adopted by using several technologies including: radio frequency, infrared, Bluetooth and mobile technologies. The customer has no need to swipe or have in their possession a credit card. The device is waived over the unit and transmitted by radio frequency to the terminal and then sent for approval to the card processor.

This is a great new technology that should appeal to retailers and consumers alike. The market is predicted to quadruple by 2006.

Chapter Twenty Four

Consumer Fraud

The major form of fraud hitting consumers and businesses is identity theft and it comes in several forms:

- **Skimming**
- **Check Fraud**
- **Cyber Crime**

According to complaints filed with the Federal Trade Commission in 2002, identity theft is the fastest growing crime in America.

The FTC reports that 43% of roughly 380,000 complaints involved stealing someone's identity, such as credit card or Social Security numbers, to commit fraud.

The top complaints by the FTC in 2002 included:

- **Identity Theft** — 43%
- **Internet Auctions** — 13%
- **Internet Service Complaints** — 6%
- **Advance Fee Loans** — 5%
- **Shop at Home Services** — 5%

A recent article by the Associated Press states that up to 700,000 people in the United States may be victimized by identity bandits each year. It costs the average victim more than $1,000 in expenses to cope with the damage to their accounts and reputations, the FTC has said.

For more research go to:

www.identitytheft.org
www.consumer.gov/idtheft
www.merchantfraudsquad.com

Lets look at the three most common forms of fraud.

Skimming

In a recent article by Daniele Micci-Barreca, Director of Fraud Solutions at ClearCommerce Corporation, he references several consumer surveys that a large percentage of potential online buyers remain highly concerned about the security of credit card transactions conducted over the Internet. The perception that credit card numbers could be compromised during the transmission between the browser and the web site, or hacked once stored in a merchant's database, limits consumer confidence in buying online. Although these risks exist, the likelihood of a card number being compromised online is relatively low because of the widespread use of SSL encryption for secure communication, firewalls and data encryption of stored information. On the other hand, few consumers consider the risk of their card numbers being compromised during face-to-face transactions by handing their cards to sales staff who often are complete strangers.

Hackers and scammers probably still find it much easier to obtain credit card numbers in the physical world because of the security measures that are in place to protect card information online. The "traditional" way to collect card numbers is "dumpster diving", basically gaining access to credit card receipts (carbon copies), which provide both credit card information and expiration dates. However, technology makes it easier for crooks to collect hundreds of credit card numbers is a much more efficient way - welcome to the world of credit card skimmers!

A skimmer is a small, self-contained device about the size of a pack of cigarettes. To avoid notice, credit card skimmers are sometimes disguised as pagers or Personal Digital Assistants (PDAs). Because of their size, they can be hidden in a pocket or behind a tie. The skimmer can read the information of a card's magnetic stripe and store up to 1,000 card numbers in memory. The unit can then be connected to a PC to download the collected information. Unfortunately, credit card skimmers are easy to find and relatively inexpensive. The web provides plenty of underground "hacker supermarkets" advertising these devices, which can be purchased for as little as $600.

The modus operandi of skimmer-based credit card fraud is quite simple and has potential when a consumer provides a credit card for payment. Skimming can occur in situations where a collusive employee temporarily takes control of the card at a point-of-sale device located out of the consumer sight. For example, a malicious restaurant waiter can quickly swipe the card through the skimmer, collecting card number and expiration date (some skimmers can also read "Track 1" data, which includes the cardholder name) while walking toward the legitimate point-of-sale terminal. This process is much easier than breaking into a corporate database to access credit card numbers online.

Because the cardholder is unaware that the card has been compromised, the number can be used for a month or two before unauthorized charges show on the cardholder statements and action is taken. Obviously, the safest place for a criminal to use these compromised numbers is on the Internet, which provides anonymous worldwide access to thousands of commerce-enabled sites. Numbers are often posted on underground chat rooms and hackers web sites for rapid exchange and distribution. To make matters worse, skimmed card numbers can be copied onto the magnetic stripes of counterfeit cards and used for face-to-face transactions.

What Merchants Can Do

What are some ways online merchants can defend themselves from credit card skimmers? One protection scheme is already present on the majority of circulating cards, particularly in the United States. The 3-digit card validation code imprinted on the back of Visa, Master Card, Discover and Diners cards and the 4-digit code imprinted in the front of American Express cards provide significant protection. Although different acronyms are used to describe these codes (CVV2, CVC2) the principle is the same. The code is not readable from the magnetic stripe and cannot be skimmed. When the consumer is asked to provide these codes in card-not-present transactions, online or by phone, a correct answer provides at least some assurance that a legitimate cardholder is using the card. To protect the effectiveness of this security mechanism, card associations mandate that online business not store the validation code in their databases, even in an encrypted format. Although card validation codes are not a complete solution to the skimming problem as the number could be annotated separately, they still provide a significant level of protection to both merchants and cardholders. For added protection, avoid storing card verification codes after the transaction has been completed and ensure that codes do not appear in web server logs or other persistent files. Fortunately, most card processors support card verification mechanisms, as part of the card authorization process and this protection is readily available to all online merchants.

For more research go to:

www.merchantfraudsquad.com

www.usa.visa.com/business/merchants/fraud_basics_index.html

Check Fraud

Check Fraud is one of the fastest growing forms of Identity theft today. Check fraud is estimated to reach $15 billion by 2004. According to several government publications, check fraud takes on multiple forms including:

- Forged signatures (legitimate blank checks with an imitation of the payor signature);
- Forged endorsements (often involving theft of a valid check, which is then endorsed and cashed or deposited by someone other than the payee);
- Counterfeit checks (the fastest-growing source of fraudulent checks, due to advances in color copying and desktop publishing capabilities);
- Altered checks (defined as valid check stock with certain information, such as the payee or written amount, changed to benefit the perpetrator);
- Check kiting (the process of depositing a check from one bank into a second bank without sufficient funds to cover it, then taking advantage of the conditional credits offered by the second bank to write a check for deposit back to the first bank to cover the original check).

For more in-depth information research the following:

www.clev.frb.org/ccca/fo1q96/fraud.htm

www.frbservices.org - To review the Federal Check Study

Check fraud, Federal Reserve System
www.frbservices.org/checks/pdf/CheckFraud.pdf

Fighting Corporate Check Fraud: Can Positive Pay Stem the Rising Tide? www.ebanklink.com/articles/positivepay.htm

How to Win the Check Fraud Game
www.ebanklink.com/stopcheckfraud/checkfraudgame.htm

www.diogenesllc.com/checkfraud.pdf

www.fbi.gov/publications.htm

Tips for Tackling Check Fraud

According to the National Check Fraud Center, check fraud and counterfeiting are among the fastest growing problems affecting the U.S. financial system. Since checks account for approximately one-third of retail spending, and they are one of the most popular forms of payment, second only to cash, retailers cannot afford to lose business by refusing to accept checks. However there are some precautions retailers can take when accepting checks that will help combat check fraud.

Here some recommendations by Telecheck for merchants to use to combat check fraud:

1. Establish a check acceptance policy detailing acceptable forms of ID, required information and dollar limits; and make no exceptions to the policy. Fraud artists are skilled at creating hassles or confusion that can leave businesses stuck with a bad check.

2. When accepting a check, make sure a name, address and phone number are printed on the check and the written and numerical dollar amounts correspond.

3. Pay attention to the "feel" of the check; most check paper has the same weight and texture.

4. Watch the check-writer sign the check. If the signature is illegible, have the customer print the name below.

5. Compare the signatures, photo and physical description of the ID with that of the check writer.

6. Check the driver's license, which should be smooth all over with no ridges that indicate an alteration or modification. Verify that the ID is still valid.

7. 90% of returned checks have low check numbers (100 to 500). While low check numbers indicate a recently opened account and a potentially more risky check, particularly for business or dab ("doing business as") checks, that is not always the case.

8. More useful information on the check is the account's opening date (month and year), usually indicated by four numbers to the side of the account holder's name and address.

9. Don't accept second-party or third-party checks (checks not made out directly to your store).

10. The four-digits following the magnetic ink character recognition (MICR) number at the bottom of the check should match the four-digit number at the top right hand of the check.

11. All checks, except government checks, should have a perforation along one side of the check.

12. You can try calling the financial institution to confirm if funds are available, but there is no guarantee that the funds will still be available when cashed or that check will clear.

Cyber Crime

Cyber Crime takes many forms, one of the most devastating is computer hacking. In a recent article Elinor Mills Abreau reports that over 8 million credit card numbers were hacked earlier this year in 2003.

A recent industry press release shows how real the threat of cyber crime is.

NEW YORK (Reuters) - The FBI is investigating a recent computer hacking incident in which as many as eight million credit card numbers may have been stolen from a company that processes transactions, industry representatives and investigators say.

In what is believed to be the biggest credit card hacking incident so far, Omaha-based Data Processors International, which processes transactions involving Visa, MasterCard, American Express and Discover Financial Services for merchants, said in a statement that it had "recently experienced a system intrusion by an unauthorized outside party."

"We are aware of the matter and looking into it," said FBI spokesman Paul Bresson, who said he could not comment further on the pending investigation.

The credit card issuing agencies said there had been no evidence that the numbers had been fraudulently used and cited "zero-liability" policies under which consumers would be protected in the case of fraud.

A MasterCard spokeswoman put the total number of credit cards exposed at around 8 million.

When news of the breach first became public on Monday, Visa and MasterCard pegged the number of credit cards exposed at 3.4 million and 2.2 million, respectively.

American Express said their number was "significantly less" than those figures, and Discover declined to give a number.

MasterCard has said it began notifying its members of the situation during the week of February 3.

"There is an epidemic of credit card theft from banks and ecommerce companies," said Alan Paller, Research Director at the Bethesda, Maryland-based System Administration, Networking and Security Institute.

Paller and David Robertson, Publishers of The Nilson Report, a credit card industry trade journal in Oxnard, California, said they believed the case was the biggest theft of credit card numbers in history.

BLACK MARKET SALES

While consumers are protected from liability, the credit card issuers will have to pay about $4 to $5 each to replace the cards, putting the total cost at between $32 million to $40 million, said Robertson.

"The real losers here are the (card) issuers themselves and potentially (Data Processors International), depending on how much insurance they have," he said. "The costs to issuers are not only just the new piece of plastic and mailing the card, but the customer service issues, such as notifying the cardholders."

Credit card institutions are prime targets for organized crime groups who try to extort money out of them and sell the card numbers on the black market, according to Paller.

In 2000 one of the first cases to became public, a hacker in Russia stole an estimated 300,000 credit card numbers from CD Universe and posted them online after the online music store refused to pay.

"These are sophisticated criminals; it's big business," Robertson said. "Credit card numbers stolen in the U.S. can end up on counterfeit cards in another part of the world."

There have also been inside jobs at credit agencies. In November, three New York men, including one who worked at a company that provides access to consumer credit information, were charged with orchestrating the largest identity theft scheme in U.S. history -- involving more than 30,000 consumers and an estimated $2.7 million in losses.

But, the data is not safe in a file drawer either, Robertson said.

"There's an illusion of safety that goes on every day. The difference with Internet hacking is the ability to crack a large database in which there are millions of accounts," he said. "This is what causes fear on the part of card issuers themselves."

Merchants and credit card companies do a good job of keeping fraud low in the United States, Robertson said. Overall, fraud has been reduced, simply by the introduction of new processes and sophisticated hardware.

Other countries do not have as many point-of-sale card authorization systems as does the U.S. and they have higher telecom costs that keep them from checking the validity of the card while the customer is waiting, he said.

"(Credit card) fraud is far worse everywhere in the world than in the United States, with the exception of France, which uses smartcards, with microchips in them," which can't be easily faked, Robertson said. "As a result, fraud in the U.S. is only 7 cents out of every $100 of sales."

Consider these basic steps to help you avoid risk and stay secure when you're online—whether you're using email or shopping at your favorite merchant.

Here are some tips from www.visa.com on buying online:

- **Protect your Visa card with Verified by Visa.** Added password protection helps ensure that only you can use your Visa card online.

- **Be discriminating when providing personal information online.** Never give out your personal or account information to anyone you do not trust. And make sure to verify a business's legitimacy by visiting its web site, calling a phone number obtained from a trusted source, and/or checking with a reliable resource such as the Better Business Bureau's BBBonline Reliability Program.

- **Keep your passwords secret.** Some online stores may require you to register with them via a user name and password before buying. Online passwords, including your Verified by Visa password, should be kept secret from outside parties the same way you protect your ATM PIN.

- **Look for signs of security.** Identify security clues such as a lock image at the bottom of your browser, or a URL that begins with https://. These signs indicate that only you and the merchant can view your payment information.

- **Never send payment information via email.** Information that travels over the Internet (such as email) is not fully protected from being read by outside parties. Most reputable merchant sites use encryption technologies that will protect your private data from being accessed by others as you conduct an online transaction.

- **Keep a record of your transaction.** Just as you save store receipts, you should keep records of your online purchases. Back up your transaction by saving and/or printing the order confirmation.

- **Review your monthly account statement thoroughly.** Immediately investigate suspicious activity to prevent any possible additional fraud before it occurs. Promptly notify your financial institution of any suspicious email activities.

For more info on cyber crime research the following:

www.fbi.gov/publications.htm

www.fbi.gov/congress/congress01/kubic061201.htm

www.cybercrime.gov

► Chapter Twenty Five ◄

Selling In The Merchant Services Industry

"Whether you think you can or that you can't, you are usually right."

- Henry Ford

There is no other industry that offers the opportunities for income, long-term security, independence and advancement that the merchant services industry does. Consider this, in most sales jobs you must hunt for prospects constantly and convince them that your service will be of benefit. In most cases you have to create the desire and the need for the product.

In our business there are prospects on every corner. Business owners know that they must accept credit cards and alternate forms of payments to be successful. Ask any retailer or Internet company where their sales would be without accepting credit cards. The question then becomes not if they are going to buy, but from whom are they going to buy?

When you have an industry where the customer knows they must have your product it creates fierce competition. Selling in the merchant services industry is competitive to say the least. Standard bankcard services have become a "me to" or commodity product. The good news that most of the competition is largely untrained, uneducated and their major marketing strategy is to sell at the cheapest price.

As industries grow and mature this is a normal occurrence. In order to thrive in this business you must be able to distinguish the value and uniqueness you provide to the merchant over the competition. There will always be someone "cheaper."

Remember, there are two types of people at any company.

- **Those That Generate Revenue**
- **Those That Consume Revenue**

Being in the sales profession puts you in the first category, just stay aware of the fact that nothing happens until something is sold. Without salespeople, banks have no merchants. Merchants don't have products to sell. Credit card processing companies don't have sales to process. Manufacturers have no way to distribute their product. Customer service departments have no customers to service. In short the economy dies.

The salesperson on the street drives this industry. Become a merchant focused salesperson; a master service provider and you will be invaluable.

Lets look at the income potential in this business.

► Chapter Twenty Six ◄

Where The Money Is

> *I bargained with Life for a penny,*
> *And Life would pay no more,*
> *However I begged at evening*
> *When I counted my scanty store;*
>
> *For Life is a just employer,*
> *And gives you what you ask,*
> *But once you have set the wages,*
> *Why, you must bear the task.*
>
> *I worked for menial's hire,*
> *Only to learn, dismayed*
> *That any wage I had asked of Life,*
> *Life would have willingly paid.*
>
> *- Jessie B. Rittenhouse*

There are several potential income streams when selling merchant services.

- **Application and Setup Fees**
- **Equipment Sales**
- **Residual Income**

Application, setup fees, and equipment sales keep the food on the table so to speak. Residual income builds slowly and continues to accumulate on a monthly basis as a merchant portfolio grows.

You need to be clear about your income goals and the actions required to reach them.

Let's look at the income potential from equipment sales. Equipment commissions vary depending on several factors:

sales price, merchant credit standing, monthly lease payment, cost of equipment and commission plan.

Commissions fluctuate depending on selling style. Some salespeople sell more terminals at lower monthly lease payments, while others will write larger leases with less volume. It all depends upon individual style and local market conditions.

A good figure to use is an average commission of $450.00 per lease. This takes into account good credit, slow credit and bad credit. Using the $450.00 commission the income potential would look like this:

Sales Week	Comm.	Monthly	Yearly
1	$450.00	$1,935.00	$23,220.00
2	$900.00	$3,870.00	$46,440.00
3	$1,350.00	$5,805.00	$69,660.00
4	$1,800.00	$7,740.00	$92,880.00
5	$2,250.00	$9,675.00	$116,100.00

As you can see the numbers can get rather large. Most full time sales representatives will average between 8-12 leases per month depending on the market area.

The number of leases that can be physically written will depend upon the office setup and support staff. Many ISOs and financial institutions now offer training and installation services to give salespeople more time to do what they do best - sell.

Residual Income

Residual income is the most powerful way to create long-term wealth. In most companies the salesperson is only as good as his last sale. With residual income you get paid monthly for a one-time effort. Servicing your merchant is critical in order to maintain your residual income base.

There are many ways residuals can be paid, here are just a few:

- **Above A Certain Buy-Rate**
- **Percentage Split**
- **Per Active Account**

Each organization pays residuals differently make sure your pay plan is understood thoroughly. Residual income is paid monthly based on the profit generated on the merchant account.

A $10.00 residual per account per month (many accounts will yield much more) and 10 new accounts per month, will earn the following on a monthly basis: (Note this is just bankcard residuals it does not take into account other residual streams from checks, gift cards etc.)

End of 1st Year (assumed 10% drop off)

    120 Accounts Sold
      12 Accounts Closed
    108 Active Accounts

    $ 1,080.00 **Monthly Residual**
    $12,960.00 **Yearly Residual**

End of 2nd Year

    108 Accounts from 1st Year
    108 New Active Accounts
    216 Total Accounts @ $10.00 each

$ 2,160.00 Monthly Residual
$25,920.00 Yearly Residual

End of 3rd Year

108 Accounts from 1st Year
108 Accounts from 2nd Year
108 New Accounts
324 Active Accounts

$ 3,240.00 Monthly Residual
$38,880.00 Yearly Residual

If you averaged just 10 sales per month your total income at the end of year three would be:

New Equipment Sales	**$54,000.00**
Residual Income	**$38,880.00**
Total Yearly Income	**$92,880.00**

I know of very few jobs where you can work hard for three years and make close to $100,000 per year – do you?

Naturally this is just an example. Your income potential is unlimited, in this business you write your own paycheck.

Many agents have a strategy of building residual income only and sell existing high volume merchants with little or no new equipment sales. These are called reprograms or rollovers. Many sales representatives can write 15-30 reprograms per month and build a significant portfolio in a relative short period of time, 18-24 months.

These projections are based one agent's efforts alone, they do not account for income that can be generated from recruiting and managing salespeople.

Organizations are always looking for people who can hire, recruit and motivate a good outside sales force. But in order to realize your income goals you must have a strategy.

► Chapter Twenty Seven ◄

What's Your Strategy?

> *"The best way to predict the future is to invent it."*
> *- Alan Kay*

Now that you are aware of the kind of income you can earn, you've got to develop a sales strategy. The best strategy is to model one that is working. Don't reinvent the wheel if you don't have to. Your strategy should be fairly simple. Try this basic outline then ask yourself the questions below so you can define a clearly defined strategy.

- **Identify your market.**
- **Analyze your market – their Needs, Wants and Problems.**
- **Satisfy their Needs, Wants and Problems – Your Products and Services.**
- **Market, Market, Market.**

Who's your market? (New businesses, existing business, auto repairs, doctors, restaurants etc.)

Are you targeting a niche?

What core products are you going to focus on offering?

Are you going to sell a bundled package or program?

How are you going to generate fresh prospects?

What tools do you need to be successful?

What skills do you need to develop?

What sales and product training do you need?

What is your Unique Selling Proposition – why are you different?

What wants, needs and problems does your product satisfy?

What benefits will your customers receive from your product?

Now, lets look at target marketing.

► Chapter Twenty Eight ◄

Target Marketing

> *"I don't measure a man's success by how high he climbs but how high he bounces when he hits bottom."*
> - Gen. George Patton

- **Prospecting is Sifting Numbers**
- **Marketing is Building Relationships**
- **Target Marketing is Focusing on The Best Prospects For Your Product**

Six key questions you need to ask when developing a target marketing strategy.

Question 1: Who? Who is my ideal prospect?
Who buys my products?
Who has a problem my product can solve?

Question 2: Where? Where do I find them?
What areas have the highest business growth?
Where can I locate this ideal prospects information?
Where can I buy or locate leads?

Question 3: What? What does my prospect want?
What challenges does my prospect face?
What's in it for them?

Question 4: Why? Why should they buy from me?
Why am I unique from the competition?

Why do they need my products or services?

Question 5: How?
How do I penetrate this market?
How do I become a specialist or expert?
What materials do I need to reach this market?
What relationships do I need to penetrate this market?

Question 6: When?
When do I begin? (How about NOW)
What is the best time to approach these prospects?
Is there a seasonal time that is best to approach this market?
Is there a better time of day to solicit this customer?

Now that you have worked on your target market, lets look at the qualities required to be an extraordinary salesperson.

▶ Chapter Twenty Nine ◀

The Extraordinary Salesperson

> *"Since most of us spend our lives doing ordinary tasks, the most important thing is to carry them out extraordinarily well."*
> - Henry David Thoreau

The sales profession is ever changing, it is dynamic. With the advent of the Internet, fierce competition and the availability of information, merchants are much more sophisticated. The extraordinary salesperson must have the ability to adapt and change strategy accordingly.

Due to the high cost of selling, many firms are reducing outside sales forces, relying on automation and inside salespeople to maintain and increase revenue. Instead of face-face contacts many companies and individuals are making their purchasing decisions directly via the Internet, direct mail, telephone, fax, radio and other means.

The exciting thing about the merchant services industry is that as more and more complex products are brought to market there will be an *increase* in the need for professional outside salespeople rather than a decline.

This new breed of salesperson must acquire skills that were not required of predecessors. The new era of selling will be as a "Partner, Consultant, or Counselor." Partnership or consultative selling means that salespeople will have to become actively engaged in their client's business. In essence they will work for them.

This new type of salesperson will be open to forgoing short-term gains in order to achieve long-term benefits. One-on-one relationships are built on a foundation of trust, respect and performance. Extraordinary salespeople form these types of partnerships with their customers. They are considered an invaluable resource.

Many companies are cutting back vendor relationships in order to deal with fewer salespeople. The consultative merchant services professional will have the ability to provide multiple solutions, benefiting their merchant and increasing streams of revenue for all parties involved. Win-win relationships will be the norm.

The days of the fast-talking, pushy, back slapping, hard closer are almost extinct. This method may continue to work in used car sales, but in the merchant services arena salespeople who use these techniques may have short-term success but are more than likely doomed to long-term failure.

Agents that have the ability to combine traditional closing methods with new sales paradigms, like value based selling, will be able to write more business without having to use high pressure tactics. Observe how successful companies market their products and services today. They focus on education, service, relationship building, and added value to the end customer.

Partnership selling entails doing things for the merchant rather than doing things to the merchant. If they don't benefit from a particular piece of equipment or service, don't sell it. The goal is to build a long-term mutually beneficial relationship, much like an accountant, lawyer or doctor has with their patients. Trust is being sold first.

The main skills for the extraordinary salesperson will not be closing, closing, closing but will emphasize building rapport, analyzing customer needs, and asking the right questions to uncover dominant buying motives. If done correctly gaining commitment will be a fluid and effortless process, not an event.

Salespeople will be required to demonstrate new qualities in order to meet the demands of today's merchant. Their makeup will include the following characteristics:

- **Integrity**
- **Authenticity**
- **Understanding**
- **Professionalism**
- **Customer Service**

Integrity is defined as a steadfast adherence to a strict moral or ethical code. The extraordinary salesperson understands that their future depends upon honesty in all business dealings. How you act demonstrates who you are much more than what you say. Integrity is demonstrated by doing what you said you were going to do, "Walking Your Talk."

Authenticity (being genuine) is the opposite of being phony. People have a second sense about whether salespeople are being real or not. Merchants know where there is a lack of a true desire to help. When being inauthentic, a salesperson's words do not match their actions or body language; customers pick up on it immediately. Be authentic in all interactions with customers.

Understanding is the ability to walk a mile in the other person's shoes. To see the wants, needs and concerns of the merchant from the merchant's perspective. There is an old saying that goes like this "If you want to see why John Smith buys look at the world through John Smith's eyes." This skill is contingent upon the ability to actively listen to the client's needs and then be able to step into their world.

By demonstrating a higher level of professionalism the extraordinary salesperson creates an environment that distinguishes them from the pack. They internalize the meaning of professionalism, which is being prepared, organized, and knowledgeable about their services and products.

They are driven by a need to serve the customer, they are merchant focused. It is understood that it cost much more to acquire a new customer than to keep an existing customer. They also realize that every customer knows roughly 250 people and if that customer isn't serviced exceptionally well their reputation will suffer.

By demonstrating these key characteristics the one-time sale will evolve into a life long partnership where all the participants win. At this stage you are a partner and partners look out for each other. Your merchants will in turn look out for you by sending referrals, buying additional products, and continuing to process with your bank.

Wrap your mind around these ideas and demonstrate them and you will be guaranteed success. Once again the main qualities of an extraordinary salesperson are:

▶ Chapter Thirty ◀

7 Reasons Why Salespeople Fail

"Defeat is not the worst of failures. Not to have tried is the true failure."
— George E. Woodberry

After working with thousands of salespeople from lackluster performers to super stars, we have heard every reason in the world why they haven't or can't succeed. We have recognized a pattern in those salespeople that do not excel in the sales profession. Many share the following characteristics:

#1 **Insufficient Product Knowledge**

#2 **They Don't Know Their Presentation**

#3 **Bad Time Management Skills**

#4 **No Marketing or Prospecting Plan**

#5 **They Didn't Research the Competition**

#6 **They Gave Up To Soon!**

#7 **They Lack Clarity About Their Purpose or Mission In Life**

It's scary that there are so many salespeople that don't thoroughly know their industry services and products. If you are going to be a professional salesperson, with the potential

©Performance Training Systems

to earn a six-figure income, you've got to learn every facet of your product line. This is a foundational key to success.

In the merchant services arena you are required to have a working knowledge of your products, services, future technologies, equipment capabilities, rates and fees, underwriting criteria, and customer service procedures. Commit to being a life long learner. Stephen Covey calls it sharpening the saw. If you continually learn and improve your skills you will soon be a master. And a master salespeople control their own destiny.

Knowing about your product in and of itself is not enough. You must be able to present your product effectively. This begins with gaining rapport, asking the right questions, discovering why your customer is buying and gaining commitment. Your presentation will require constant tweaking and improvement to perfect. Try new things, test different approaches until the right one is discovered.

Bad time management skills are one of the biggest killers of sales success. Poor salespeople don't manage their time they let outside circumstances control their destiny. Time is the only finite resource we have, use your time wisely, prioritize and spend time on those activities that generate revenue.

You've heard it before "People don't plan to fail, they fail to plan." You must have a prospecting and marketing plan that is executed daily. **Guess what? Selling is a contact sport you have got to suit up and show up everyday.** It all begins with finding an interested party. Create a system that utilizes multiple lead channels, this will ensure you're never without a prospect to call on. One of the best buying signals is that a merchant will listen to you.

You must research your competition. Make sure you know who all your major competitors are, call and shop them. File a new business DBA and see what mailers you receive. Research their rates, their selling strategy, what sales tools they are using and promotions they are offering. Learn their strengths and weaknesses so you can capitalize on them at every turn.

> *A Quitter **NEVER** wins – and a **WINNER** never Quits!*
> *- Source Unknown*

This is the worst one of all. You won't believe the number of salespeople that fold their tents up to early. Many of us have expectations of becoming successful but forget the work and persistence required to realize our goals. Give yourself enough time to learn your trade. Dedicate six months to this industry and you will never leave.

The final reason most salespeople, and people for that matter fail is that they lack clarity about their life mission or purpose. A big part of a person's life is spent working. Your career should be a key ingredient in fulfilling you purpose on this planet. Alignment of values, mission and goals is a critical step in achieving your destiny. If these factors are not in alignment you're what is called incongruent.

> *"There is one quality which one must possess to win, and that is definiteness of purpose, the knowledge of what one wants and a burning desire to possess it."*
> *- Napoleon Hill*

Many people divide their life between what they feel they have to do to make a living and what they want to do to have fun or gain fulfillment.

For instance you may have a goal of making $100,000 per year and another goal of working 30 hours a week and spending more time with your family. This is a conflicting goal initially because you will have to spend more than 30 hours a week building your business until your business network grows. You are incongruent. It's been said to "work smart not hard." in the beginning why not "work hard and smart."

Do what you love and love what you do. Naturally, there are always elements, even in things we love, that we may not care for. Just ensure that this business offers you more of what you love to do than what you don't.

I can't urge you enough to explore how your business will help you accomplish your life purpose. It will help you gain clarity on where you are going and how you're going to get there. In order to explore your business mission and values I invite you to complete a workshop. You may download the life design workshop at our website free of charge www.surviveandthrive.biz

Remember what Nietzsche said:

"If the WHY is strong enough, you can bear and HOW"

► Chapter Thirty One ◄

The Sales Process

> "Do, or do not. There is no try."
> - Yoda

The sales process is not an event. It is a fluid movement from one step to the next. It should be natural and unforced. Here are the steps involved:

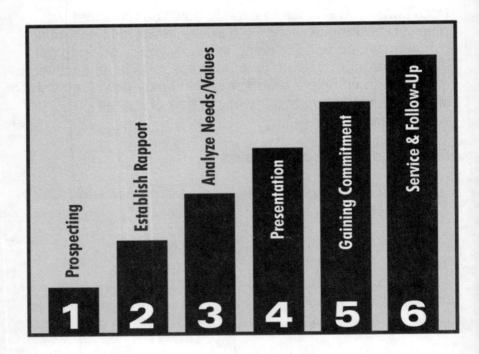

Lets review each step in detail.

► Chapter Thirty Two ◄

Prospecting

"One who has a thing to sell, and goes and whispers in a well, is not so apt to get the dollars, as one who climbs a tree and hollers"
- Chinese Proverb

I once heard it said *"that you can have the best story in the world, but if you don't have anyone to tell it to – it's useless."* New business development is paramount to your success.

Your marketing and prospecting plan should outline the steps that need to be taken to generate sufficient leads to reach your sales goals. Make sure you develop a prospecting strategy that fits your personality and individual style. If you know you are not going to cold call, don't lie to yourself, develop and alternate strategy.

Here are several tactics to generate solid prospects.

- Cold Calling
- Telemarketing
- Niche or Target Marketing (i.e. restaurants, doctors, car dealerships)
- Direct Mail
- Referrals and/or Joint Ventures
- Lead Companies
- Internet Websites
- Association Endorsements
- Chamber of Commerce Meetings
- Lead Exchange Groups
- Civic Groups

- Seminars
- Print Media
- Free Reports
- Free Email Course
- Free Newsletter
- Free Ebooks
- Recorded Sizzle Message
- Auto Dialing Machines
- Tele-classes
- Coupons
- Trade Shows
- Local Newspapers
- Picture Business Card
- Vacation Vouchers

Lets review each method in detail.

Tactic #1 - Cold Calling

Cold Calling – New Businesses

Cold calling is still one of the most effective ways to reach prospects. The advantage of marketing to new businesses is that they must accept credit cards and they need equipment. The disadvantage of marketing to new businesses is that every merchant service provider is going after this market. The new business market is huge, according to info USA there are over 50,000 new businesses started each week in the United States.

If approaching new businesses you will need to acquire a new business list. This can usually be done through a list company such as www.infousa.com or the most affordable route is usually the local county court house. Just inquire about the new business list, corporation's list or assumed names, the wording varies by state. Many agencies will fax or email the list daily or weekly for a fee.

Once the list is acquired, target only those merchants that require your product or service (use some common sense). Sort them by zip code so a route can be developed. While on the road look for signs like "Grand Opening", "Under New Management" and "Coming Soon."

If your list has phone numbers the most effective approach is to call and set appointments, this will save time and money in your prospecting efforts.

If you would like to figure out how many cold calls you need to make to reach a certain annual income complete the **Income Goal Worksheet in Appendix A.**

A good beginning ratio for cold calling is a 10% presentation ratio and a 20% closing ratio. If you make 50 cold calls a day you will get 5 presentations and close 1 sale.

Cold Calling – Existing Businesses

Existing business are always looking to improve the bottom line. Rather than leading with traditional merchant services you may want to lead with a tier I or II product. Try opening the door with one of the following

- **Debit Services**
- **Gift Cards**
- **Loyalty Cards**
- **Payroll Card**
- **Prepaid Product**
- **Check Guarantee**

- **Check Conversion**
- **Internet Processing**
- **Website Design**

Another tactic is to make a service call. You can open a dialogue with a merchant by giving him new stickers or cleaning the heads on his credit card terminal.

The best plan is to decide the night before which area you will target. If targeting existing businesses work the areas that have the most businesses. North, East, West, South it doesn't matter there are merchants everywhere.

You may find existing business lists from:

- www.goleads.com
- www.delorme.com (Xmap Package)
- www.infousa.com
- www.thomasregister.com
- The Yellow Pages
- Hoovers Online
- Thompson Manufacturers Directory

Target those businesses that use credit cards the most. Such as, auto repairs, carpet stores, furniture stores, restaurants, retailers, car dealerships, doctors, dentist, repair and service companies.

Tactic #2 - Telemarketing

Telemarketing is a great source for generating qualified prospects. More people can be contacted in less time on the phone than face-to-face. Another great strategy is to hire a part time telemarketer on commission. Get a list, develop a script and have them hit the phones.

©Performance Training Systems

Many people today want to work from home. This is a win-win situation for everyone involved. A good telemarketer is worth there weight in gold. Call the new business list yourself unless your telemarketer is experienced. New business leads are valuable, inexperienced telemarketers can burn through a lot of good leads until they get proficient on the phone.

Remember when telemarketing that the appointment is being sold not the product. Once the appointment is set you may want to qualify your prospect in more detail. Making sure they have their business banking setup and that all decision makers will be at the appointment.

You may want to offer an inducement or bonus for meeting with you, like a free business planning software package, free ebook, free report, a waiver of all application or setup fees, a free printer, try several different promotions.

Telephone surveys are another great tool to determine merchant interest. Conduct a one-minute survey and call those merchants later in the week who expressed an interest in saving money.

Here are some basic tips for successful telemarketing:

1. Before placing a call, have a clear, specific objective of what you are trying to achieve. Know the purpose of your call in advance.

2. To stay on track and meet your objective, prepare a list of questions, requiring answers, prior to your call. Have a prepared script, with all the possible answers to objections until you get comfortable on the phone.

3. Calling into multiple departments in a company or organization can not only provide the information or

person sought, but also give a unique overview of how a company's internal processes work. This can be useful information if further calls are required to the same or similar companies. Human Resources, Purchasing, Investor Relations or the President's office are all good examples of places to begin the initial foray.

4. By starting at the top of an organization such as the President's office, the President or assistant will know the correct source of information or the individual who can provide what is needed to meet the objective. As these individuals are usually very busy, having a short concise statement prepared such as "who is responsible for..." enables them to provide a quick answer.

5. When being referred from a higher-level person (such as the President or their office) to a lower level person, use the higher person's name or office to lend credibility and importance to the request. For example: "Mr. Smith's office referred me to you regarding <the nature of the call>."

6. After briefly introducing yourself and your company, ask for permission to speak, before explaining the reason of the call.

7. If the person sounds busy, make an appointment by asking when would be a good time to schedule a call.

8. Use the optional choice methodology. Ask which is better, Monday or Tuesday? Morning or afternoon? 10:00 or 11:00 a.m.? The result will be a person who is expecting the call.

9. Listen to what is going on in the background. If a call or distraction occurs in the background, politely

inquire whether or not that situation needs to be dealt with and offer to be placed on hold. This shows respect for the other person and is greatly appreciated.

10. Practice the Q/A/F/Q technique. Ask a Question. Wait for an answer. Feed back what was said to you to be sure you have a clear understanding of what was said. Finally ask another Question to direct the conversation into the area where you want it to go. The person asking the questions controls the direction of the call.

11. Finally, and most important, be persistent in your quest. If you remain persistent, you will most likely find the person who has the information you seek.

Need help developing the right telemarketing script? Go to **Developing a Telemarketing Script in Appendix C.**

Tactic #3 - Niche or Target Marketing

Many successful salespeople specialize in niche or target markets. For instance you may want to specialize in just restaurants or doctors. If you're in a niche market you need to possess a complete knowledge of that particular market and how your products will uniquely benefit the merchant. Review the chapter on target marketing for ideas.

Get involved with local associations, write free articles, advertise in their newsletters or publications and speak at their meetings. Try to get involved on the national level and create a special merchant program for their association.

Have your merchants write you testimonial letters. Align with key suppliers who work with that market. If you are selling to

---
©Performance Training Systems

restaurants get with other equipment vendors, consultants, menu designers and develop cross referral relationships.

Become the expert. Make sure you service these customers above and beyond. A niche market is a double-edged sword. Merchants know each other if you don't service your merchant the word will get out.

Tactic #4 - Direct Mail

Direct mail is still a fairly good source for leads. If you filed a DBA as we recommended earlier you will know who is actively mailing in your market area.

Make you are getting a good return on your investment. For example, if mailing 4,000 pieces per month the postage alone is $920.00 plus printing, labels, list cost and time. The average return is a 1%-2% response depending on the area and sales copy.

That means that a 4,000 piece mailing with at 1% response will generate 40 calls. The presentation ratio should be much higher with call-ins, usually around 30-40%. That means a good representative will get in front of 16 people and close 30%+ of those appointments.

Another tactic is a pre-approach letter. Send out an introduction letter before you call your customer. This works well when targeting niche markets, but the cost is high.

Always track responses and closing ratios in order to determine if your return on investment.

Tactic #5 - Referrals And Joint Ventures

Referrals continue to be one of the best sources for leads. Offer customers and business associates a referral fee for each sale. If delivering and training on a new installation always ask for five referrals before leaving.

Here are some great types of businesses to look for referral partnerships:

- Advertising Reps
- Alarm System Companies
- CPA's
- Consultants
- Financial Planners
- Hosting Companies
- Insurance Agents
- Local Banks
- MLM Distributors
- Newspapers
- Office Equipment Reps
- Payroll Sales Reps
- Printing Companies
- Restaurant Sales Reps
- Sign Companies
- Software Sales Companies
- Telecom Sales Reps
- Trade Journals
- Web Site Designers

If you build a referral network big enough you will never have to make a cold call again.

Tactic #6 – Lead Companies

A lead companies job is to generate the appointment or lead for sale. Lead companies help salespeople concentrate their efforts on selling. The drawbacks are expense and sometimes quality. Often when buying leads the first couple of batches are great, but then the lead quality drops off. Expect to pay between $7.00 - $15.00 per lead. Check out www.buyerzone.com and www.respond.com for leads.

There are also telemarketing centers that will pre-set appointments. They usually work on a set amount of appointments per week and require prepayment. Prices range from $25.00-$50.00 each appointment. Some will work out a fee arrangement for a lower appointment fee with a bonus per sale or a joint venture agreement.

Always monitor lead quality.

Tactic #7 – Internet Websites

The Internet is a great source of advertising. Competition on the Internet is fierce. You must have a fairly sizable budget to advertise successfully on the Internet. Payperclick search engines are getting more and more popular. These search engines allow the website owner to advertise their site at the top of the search engine for a fee. The largest fee based service is www.overture.com, another popular place is www.payperclicksearchengines.com.

You must have a website, hosting company and email address before getting started. Always check with the bank there may be design guidelines that need to be met before advertising.

Make sure to offer an affiliate program. Affiliate programs offer other website owners or businesses a commission to send you a potential buyer.

Tactic #8 – Association Endorsements

Association endorsements are about the best lead source available. If selected as the vendor of choice for a large association, success is assured.

The only challenge is that larger associations have agreements in place and the sales cycle is very long to land these types of accounts.

Only spend 5%-10% of your time dealing with associations or trade groups, but if you get one, that business can produce tremendous income.

Tactic #9 – Chamber of Commerce Meetings

Chamber of commerce meetings are a great place to meet business owners. Join your local chamber and attend all meetings and start to earn new referral business.

Members receive 2-3 minutes at each meeting to introduce your products and services. Most chambers also have social mixers where you can network with other members.

Chambers also publish periodic newsletters and journals featuring new members. Offer to write an article in your local chamber newsletter it will give you great exposure.

Tactic #10 – Lead Exchange Groups

A lead exchange group is comprised of non-competitive businesses that exchange leads. Lead exchange groups usually meet once every two weeks or so.

A great lead exchange group is BNI they are located at www.bni.com. If you don't have a lead exchange group in your market area, start one.

Tactic #11 - Civic Groups

There are many civic groups and organizations available that will benefit you personally and professionally. Here are just a few:

- **Toast Masters**
- **PTO/PTA**
- **Kiwanis Club**
- **Professional Associations**
- **Red Cross**
- **Networking Groups**
- **Elks**
- **Habitat for Humanity**
- **Rotary Club**
- **Lions Club**
- **Optimist Club**
- **VFW**
- **YMCA/YWCA**
- **Church Groups**
- **Sports Leagues**
- **Charity Groups**

Tactic #12 - Seminars

Seminars are a great way to promote any business. The ideal situation would be to get a group of complementary companies together to share in the expense.

Many new business owners want information on starting, expanding or growing their business. You may want to partner up with a website company, hosting company, printer, office equipment vendors or CPA and offer a small business seminar.

©Performance Training Systems

Seminars may also be conducted at business expos and trade shows.

Tactic #13 – Print Media

Print advertising is a great source for leads if you have the budget. Some great sources for advertising are the local yellow pages, magazines, trade journals and newsletters.

Check circulation and readership numbers to make sure you are getting a good value for each advertising dollar. There are thousands of trade journals available at affordable rates.

A live person is recommended for answering the phone at all times when advertising in print media. Many people want information immediately and will not leave a message on a voice mail system. If you must use a voice mail system have caller id installed in order to track hang-ups.

Tactic #14 - Free Reports

One great lead tactic is to create a free report (i.e. 10 Keys to Avoiding Credit Card Fraud, 7 Things You Should Know Before Setting Up a Merchant Account) and give away to prospective merchants at no charge. Free reports give value and open the door to begin a sales dialogue.

Tactic #15 - Free Email Course

Create a free email course for prospective merchants (i.e. The 5 steps to Increasing Sales with Credit Cards). You can set this up with a system called an auto responder. Many auto responder services are free go to www.getresponse.com/index/45256 to see how they work.

Basically, write the course and load it into your auto responder. The auto responder will automatically deliver the emails to the customer 24 hours a day 7 days a week. Auto responders also allow the delivery of multiple emails over a specified period of time. The great thing is that once the course is written it never has to be touched again.

Put the free course offering on all mailings and business cards and you now have an automated salesperson working for you 24 hours a day.

Tactic #16 – Free Newsletter

This one will take a little more effort and time on your part. Newsletters are a great way to introduce new products or services.

I would recommend an email newsletter. For a free list manager go to www.ezinemanager.com. Newsletters can be sent out bi-weekly or monthly and it's a great way to stay in touch with your customer base.

Tactic #17 – Free Ebooks

Ebook giveaways are great prospecting tools, sales closers and bonus offerings. You can give away several useful titles such as:

- **How to Write a Business Plan**
- **Magic Letters**
- **7 Secrets to Unlimited Traffic**
- **Scientific Advertising**
- **Online Business Primer**
- **Magnetic Internet Power Marketing**
- **Great Internet Secrets**
- **Unlimited Profits**

- **Discover How to Write Killer Ads**
- **The Magic Story**
- **Absolute Beginners Guide to Starting a Website**
- **Ebay Marketing Secrets**
- **Wholesale Sources Directory**
- **Million Dollar Emails**
- **Working with Clickbank**
- **Auto Responder Magic**
- **Millionaire Marketing**
- **An Easy Guide to Self-publishing Ebooks**

All of these titles can be purchased for a one-time fee of $44.95. You have full re-sale rights, which means you can giveaway or sell an infinite number of copies of each ebook.

This is an affordable way to increase your prospecting efforts for a small investment. Use them to differentiate yourself from the competition.

You can deliver these products on floppies, cds, dvds, printed or from a website download.

If you are interested in purchasing these ebooks go to www.bankcard101.com

Tactic #18 – Recorded Sizzle Message

Let's borrow a tool from the MLM industry. This is a very cost-effective means of advertising. Rent a toll free voice mail number for roughly $9.95 per month and record a 3-minute infomercial about your products and services. Many times prospects don't want to call the number off your direct mail piece because they know they are going to be sold. This method allows them to listen to a sizzle message and then have the option to leave their name and number.

Some systems offer multiple voice mail boxes and fax on demand capabilities so you can auto fax brochures to your customers. We have found an affordable one at www.fvsystems.com/20067

Tactic #19 – Auto Dialing Equipment

Almost everyone has been called by an auto-dialer, 99.9% of the people called hang-up, but the other .01% respond. Verify if auto dialers are legal in your state and what the requirements are before implementing.

A 4-line auto dialer can reach up to 4,000 businesses per day. Naturally you need to be in a market area large enough so the same people are not being called over and over. I would suggest a market population of at least 300,000+ people.

Tactic #20 – Tele-classes

Offer a free or fee based tele-class for new merchants about accepting credit cards, check and debit. At the end of the tele-class you can offer your services or give them your contact information.

Tele-classes are more cost effective than regular seminars because it is done over the phone. Here is a website where you can get a free conference call line at www.freeconference.com.

Tactic #21 - Coupons

Consumers love coupons. Create a coupon for a Free Application fee, Free Setup, Referral Fee, Free Printer, One Hour of Free Consulting, anything you can think of. Offer this coupon when cold calling or as a bonus for doing business with your company.

Tactic #22 – Trade Shows

Trade shows are great places to find new customers and develop partnerships with compatible businesses. Look for local trade shows or business expos in your area. Chambers often put on a yearly trade show.

For a listing of trade shows nationally go to: www.tradeshowbiz.com or at www.tsnn.com

Tactic #23 – Local Newspapers

Check your local newspapers, business journals and weekly papers. Many will list new businesses just starting and businesses moving to the area.

Call all the businesses advertising with no credit card logos in the local papers, service directories and offer services.

For business leads go to www.bizjournals.com.

Tactic #24 – A Picture Business Card

This tactic has served the real estate business well. The business card is your representation of who you are to the business community. Since most people are visual, they remember other people's faces. A business card with a picture has ten times the impact of a normal card.

Also, use the back of the card. Write out all the hot buttons or benefits on the back of the card. Use your card as an advertising tool that moves your customer to action.

Tactic #25 – Free Vacation Vouchers

Vacation vouchers have been used for years to help generate leads. You can offer them as a bonus when a sale is made or just to make a presentation. They are also great tools to increase response on your direct mail pieces.

Note: You will not have time to utilize all 25 prospecting tactics. Choose 3-5 tactics and implement them on a consistent basis and you will have a full pipeline of prospects to sell to.

©Performance Training Systems

Chapter Thirty Three

The Science of Rapport

"If you would win a man to your cause, first convince him that you are his sincere friend"
- *Abraham Lincoln*

Establishing rapport is the most critical factor in the sales process. Without a rapport the odds of making a sale are slim and none. Rapport is achieved when two people can see the other person's viewpoint, be on the same wavelength, and appreciate each other's situation.

One technology that has helped me (Marc B) tremendously is NLP - Neuro Linguistic Programming. NLP was originally the creation of Richard Bandler and John Grinder who, in the early 1970s, combined their computer programming and linguistic skills to develop a new model of how to produce positive change in human beings.

Neuro refers to the physiological processes associated with internal pictures, sounds and feelings. Linguistic refers to the language associated with those internal experiences. Programming refers to the fact that we have choices, that once we understand our own (and others) internal maps, we can choose to change them or reprogram them and thus change the way we experience the world.

NLP is a model of excellence; it has provided a roadmap for successful therapists, salespeople, communicators, and business people. NLP is a kind of human "software" that can be used to organize your experiences in more productive ways.

I will include several exercises in the Appendices that will help you generate new behaviors and overcome limiting beliefs. But, first let's look at what rapport really means.

Here's a great acronym for Rapport:

- **R** eally
- **A** ll
- **P** eople
- **P** refer
- **O** thers
- **R** esembling
- **T** hemselves

The standard definition of rapport is a relation of harmony, conformity, accord or affinity. Rapport is the central organizing concept for any communication interaction. If you don't have rapport your customer will not purchase. When you have rapport it creates an atmosphere of:

- **Trust**
- **Confidence**
- **Participation**

The benefit of rapport is the establishment of **SAMENESS** the moving together in a common direction. **DIFFERENCE** is the basis of poor rapport.

Notice when people are in rapport – there is a pattern or dance to their communication and interaction. Their rhythm, bodies and words match each other.

Remember when communicating, people process the majority of their information through three of their five senses. People use all five strategies, but primarily use one particular strategy for processing information internally.

They primarily utilize one of the following senses:

Visual	=	**Mental Pictures (Most People)**
Auditory	=	**Sound or Internal Dialogue**
Kinesthetic	=	**Feelings or Emotions**

How do you tell if a person is visual, auditory or kinesthetic? Listen to their language, here are the most common predicates (verbs, adverbs, and adjectives) people use and their representational system:

Visual	**Auditory**	**Kinesthetic**
see	sound	feel
picture	hear	relax
perceive	discuss	grasp
notice	listen	handle
look	talk	stress
show	call on	pressure
appear	quiet	smooth
clear	inquire	clumsy
pretty	noisy	rough
colorful	loud	hard
hazy	outspoken	grip
flash	scream	rush
focus	pronounce	firm
bright	remark	euphoric
scene	resonate	clammy
perspective	harmony	touch
imagine	shrill	calm

view	oral	dull
vista	whimper	burning
horizon	mention	stinging
make a scene	tongue-tied	get the drift
tunnel vision	ring a bell	boils down to
plainly see	loud and clear	hang in there
see eye-to-eye	idle talk	sharp as a tack
mind's eye	to tell the truth	slipped my mind
bright future	word for word	pull some strings
in the light of	unheard of	smooth operator

Most people mis-communicate because they process information differently. By understanding how your customer processes information you can use the words that work best for them to explain your products and services. This establishes rapport.

For instance, if I have a kinesthetic (feeling) merchant, I don't want to show him a picture of a terminal. I want to hand him a terminal so he can actually feel and touch the unit. If I don't have a demo unit – I might use phrases like "this is a really solid unit" or "its sturdy construction means less service problems down the road."

It may feel awkward at first, but trust me it works.

Here are some other clues for determining a person's representational system:

Visual (Seeing)

Eyes: These people look up to there right or left, or their eyes may appear unfocused

Gestures: include pointing	Their gestures are quick, angular, and
Breathing & Speech:	High, shallow and quick
Words:	See, look, imagine, perspective, reveal
Presentations:	Prefer pictures, diagrams, movies

Hearing (Auditory)

Eyes:	These people look down to the left and may appear "shifty-eyed"
Gestures:	Rhythmic, touching face (rubbing chin)
Breathing & Speech:	Mid-chest, rhythmic
Words:	Hear, listen, ask, tell, clicks, in-tune
Presentations:	Prefer lists, summarize, quote, read

Feeling (Kinesthetic)

Eyes:	These people look down to the right
Gestures: chest	Their gestures are rhythmic, touching
Breathing & Speech:	Deep, slow with pauses
Words:	Feel, touch, grasp, catch on, contact

Presentations: They prefer hands-on, do-it demonstrations, test drive

What's Your Representational Style?

For each of the following questions, go with the first answer that comes to mind.

1. When you think of your first car, what comes to mind first?

    a. A picture, i.e. you driving your car?
    b. A sound, i.e. the sound of the car starting up?
    c. A touch, i.e. the way the car handled?
    d. A smell, i.e. the smell of the interior?
    e. A taste, i.e. food you ate in the car?

2. When you think about something funny, what is the first thing that comes to mind?

    a. A sound, i.e. a joke you heard?
    b. A smell
    c. An emotion, i.e. someone tickling you?
    d. A taste
    e. An image or picture i.e. a comic telling a joke?

3. When you think about your favorite restaurant, what do you think of first?

    a. A picture, i.e. the furniture? the people?
    b. A taste, i.e. your favorite dish there?
    c. A smell, i.e. the aroma of the kitchen?
    d. A sound, i.e. the owner saying hello?
    e. A touch, i.e. how you feel when you are there?

4. When you think about your job, what comes to mind first?

   a. An emotion, i.e. how you feel about your job?
   b. A sound, i.e. people talking in the office?
   c. A taste?
   d. An image, i.e. you sitting at your desk?
   e. A smell, i.e. something in the environment?

5. When you think back on your last birthday, what comes to mind?

   a. A taste, i.e. something you ate?
   b. A smell, i.e. the candles burning on the cake?
   c. A picture, i.e. where you had the party? the balloons?
   d. A sound, i.e. people singing "Happy Birthday"?
   e. A touch, i.e. someone hugging you?

6. When you think about your next vacation, what do you think about first?

   a. An image, i.e. the beach? skiing? scuba diving?
   b. A sound, i.e. the family laughing or playing?
   c. A smell, i.e. the food at the buffet?
   d. A touch, i.e. the warm sun on your skin?
   e. A taste, i.e. an ice cold drink?

7. When you think about a physically challenging activity, what do you think of first?

   a. A sound, i.e. a conversation you have with yourself?
   b. A touch, i.e. how the weights feel in you hand?
   c. A smell?
   d. A taste?
   e. A picture or image, i.e. seeing yourself exercising?

©Performance Training Systems

8. When you think about a major challenge you have had in your life, what comes to mind first?

    a. An image or picture, i.e. you going through the challenge?
    b. A sound, i.e. someone speaking to you?
    c. A touch, i.e. an emotion you felt?
    d. A taste?
    e. A smell?

9. When you think about your mother, what comes to mind first?

    a. A picture, i.e. what she looks or looked like?
    b. A touch or emotion, i.e. how she hugged you?
    c. A smell, i.e. her perfume?
    d. A taste, i.e. her cooking?
    e. A sound, i.e. her calling you in for dinner?

10. When you think about your favorite book, what do you think of first?

    a. A taste, i.e. what you were eating while reading?
    b. A smell?
    c. An image, i.e. the book cover? the characters?
    d. An emotion, i.e. how you felt while reading?
    e. A sound, i.e. you talking to yourself?

Review your answers and determine what representational system you lean on the most. Also determine the one you use the least, this will be the style that needs more work when attempting to develop rapport with that type of person.

Another great tool for establishing rapport is called mirroring. This is when you mirror your customer's posture, gestures, tonality and breathing (this is not mimicking – it is just flowing with them).

Mirroring occurs naturally when two people are in rapport. Just go to a mall or nightclub and watch people in deep communication they are already mirroring each other. They might lean in when speaking or have their legs crossed the same way, or they may be making the same hand gestures, etc.

Mirroring is not a gimmick it is a valuable tool designed to help you enter your customers world and get "in sync" with their wants, needs and desires.

Studies show that during interpersonal communication a major part of communication is through body language and verbal tonality. Use every tool available.

Here are several tips on building rapport:

- **Match the type of words the client uses**
- **Follow their pace**
- **Listen for inflection, match their tone**
- **Mirror their posture, gestures and breathing**

Think back to a time when you were in rapport with someone, maybe a close friend or loved one, and examine how you were interacting. Weren't you both speaking at the same pace, using relatively the same movements and gestures?

People buy from people they like. Getting into rapport with your merchants is a critical step in the sales process. If you don't have rapport, stop and regain rapport and continue. Practice rapport-building skills with everyone your meet, after awhile it will become second nature.

Chapter Thirty Four

Analyzing Needs and Uncovering Buying Values

> *"You can tell whether a man is clever by his answers. You can tell whether a man is wise by his questions."*
> *- Naguib, Mahfouz*

This is one of the most critical stages of the sales process.

During this phase you should be listening 80% of the time and talking 20% of the time. Top sales producers actively listen much more than they speak. The way we learn about our customer's needs and expectations is by asking questions. A conversation begins a sales dialogue.

Questions serve many purposes:

- **You learn valuable information about your customer and their situation.**

- **They relieve pressure.**

- **By asking a question you can be sure that they understand your point, especially when dealing with a complicated issue.**

- **The answers to your questions help you judge the progress you are making in your presentation.**

Remember, you are on a fact-finding mission. Find out what *their* expectations are in a payment system, a new vendor relationship or your service.

The initial questions asked are determined by the service or product you are marketing. Our goal is to get the initial information we need to recommend the right solution and then finish up with the three value questions in order to determine their dominant buying motive.

There are many different types of questions you can ask:

Open-Ended questions: (informational)

Who, What, Where, When, How?

Closed-Ended questions: (answer is usually a yes or no)

Would you consider changing processors if I could save you _____ in fees?

Emotional: How do you feel about....?

Preference: Which to you prefer....?

Trial Close: Is this what you were looking for?

Tie-Downs: This is important to you isn't it?

Make sure you know all the questions you are going to ask during the initial interview stage.
If you can't remember them create a client questionnaire (there is a sample one for you in Appendix D). Naturally your questions will be determined by your sales call goal.

By really listening to your merchant's answers you are demonstrating the qualities of an extraordinary salespersons. This is your greatest tool to establish rapport and trust. Who do people like to talk about the most? You guessed it – themselves. Get them talking about their plans and aspirations.

Once you have investigated their business plan, work your way into the three value questions. These three value questions will determine the customer's dominant buying motive.

Use your own language style to ask these questions, these are just examples.

    1. Mr. Merchant (first name) what is <u>MOST</u> important to you when considering the purchase of a payment system (whatever product your selling)?

OR

    Mr. Merchant what is most important to you when considering a new vendor?

    2. How do you know when you have_____?

We want the merchant's definition of what is most important; don't assume you know what service, price or quality means, have them define it.

    3. If I could show you a program that gives you_____, and make sense for you, not me, would you consider doing business today?

OR

If I could give you_____ would you feel comfortable moving forward?

©Performance Training Systems

If the client responds "No" ask, "What else is important to you when purchasing a payment system?" and repeat the cycle.

By asking these questions you are uncovering your customer's dominant buying values. Now you know what is important to them, make sure you highlight their buying values throughout the presentation.

Example:

Salesperson:	Mr. Merchant, what is MOST important to you when considering the purchase of a payment system?
Merchant:	I would have to say service.
Salesperson:	Mr. Merchant, how do you know when you have great service?
Merchant:	Well that's easy there is someone on the other end of the phone when I call. I don't have time to make 5 calls to get an answer to my question.
Salesperson:	Mr. Merchant, let me ask you a question, if I could show you a program that offered great service, and makes sense for you not me, would you considering doing business today?
Merchant:	Sure, I'd consider it.

By asking the value questions you already have your merchant moving in the right direction – towards a sale. Everybody is different use these questions as a template, work on the wording to fit your individual style.

Questions are the doorway to your customers mind, take the time upfront to explore their world and you will eliminate most of the roadblocks before the occur.

▶ Chapter Thirty Five ◀

The Presentation

> *"The path to success is to take massive, determined action."*
> *- Anthony Robbins*

Up to this point we have gained rapport and hopefully uncovered the most important factors in your merchant's buying decision process. Now is the time to demonstrate that you can meet their requirements.

Here are 6 keys to making successful presentations:

Key #1 Be Enthusiastic

The definition of enthusiasm is a source or cause of great excitement or interest. The quality that will lift your presentation above all others is the enthusiasm you have for your products and services. Without enthusiasm yours is just another sales story, the kind that merchants forget the minute you walk out the door.

Enthusiasm comes from a genuine passion about what you do, and how you feel you will positively impact your customer. Transfer your enthusiasm to your customers, this is your only chance to make a lasting impression and win the sale with this merchant. Enthusiasm is contagious and it sells.

Think about it, have you ever purchased a product or service because of the sales persons sheer exuberance? Have you given your business to the person that genuinely wanted to help you?

©Performance Training Systems

People have a sixth sense, no amount of enthusiasm will work if you don't believe in the benefits of what your offering. If you're sold on your company, services and products you will generate genuine enthusiasm.

Key #2 – Be Prepared

Make sure you know your presentation from start to finish. Video tape and record your presentation, look for any flaws, gaps or information missing.

Focus on benefits, not features.

- **A Feature represents an aspect of your product or service. A Feature explains what your product does.**

- **Benefits represent what that feature provides. How it will make life easier for the merchant or their customer.**

Tune into your customers radio station **WIIFM** and answer this question for them.

WIIFM = What's in it for ME?

Work with an experienced agent in your sales office. Have other agents give you their presentation. Call your competitors and see how they sell their products.

Keep a notebook and take notes after every presentation. Analyze what went right and what went wrong? Always look for ways to improve your presentation skills.

Key #3 Create a Powerful Opening Introduction

Most presentations begin with an introduction about the salesperson and the company you represent. This is your first opportunity after establishing rapport to really impact your prospect. **You won't get a second chance to make a first impression.**

Make sure you use your prospect's fist name at least once in the introduction and throughout your presentation. Your opening introduction should be an attention grabber that demonstrates the major benefits or unique selling proposition of your company. The introduction may also be used to prevent a common objection before it is raised.

Here's a sample traditional introduction:

Mr. Merchant (use their first name) I'd like to start by thanking you for your time, I know it's valuable. I have been specializing in helping merchants reduce overhead and increase sales, sometimes up to 50% for several years now. I feel like one of our unique benefits is that we are a local company representing one of the largest processors of financial transactions in the country. We offer one stop shopping for all your financial services including check processing, gift and loyalty cards, debit and credit card processing. I feel we are uniquely qualified to partner with your company and meet all your transaction processing needs. I'd like to start by asking you a few questions so I can recommend the right solution? How's that sound?

Low Pressure Model:

Mr. Merchant (use their first name) I'd like to start by thanking you for your time, I know it's valuable. The first thing I think you should know about our company is our method of working with merchants is a little different from our competitors. We don't use any high-pressure sales tactics, tricks or gimmicks to force you to do business with us. Often traditional sales methods cause unwanted pressure on our customers and quite frankly on me. And a lot of times it turns into an adversarial relationship. So I just want to begin by saying, "relax", I'm here to create a win-win relationship for both of us. I'm not here to sell you anything. But I am here to create an atmosphere where you can buy without being pressured. Does that sound fair enough? Great

I'd like to start by asking you a couple of questions so I can get a clear picture of what you needs are, okay?

Try several different variations and see what works best for you. Make your introduction personal, if you have 15 years in the retail business or a unique background emphasize it in your introduction and explain how that will benefit your merchant.

Memorize your introduction it's got to be fluid and smooth.

Key #4 – Use Vivid Words

Paint a clear and vivid picture for your merchant. Review Chapter 33 – The Science of Rapport.

If you haven't figured out their strategy, hit them all. Work all three into your presentation. Remember a picture is worth a thousand words; don't forget roughly 60% of all people are visual.

Design a presentation book that you can refer to while speaking to your merchant. Use colorful graphics, charts and articles to highlight major selling points. This method works well; it keeps their mind busy while you are speaking to them. It also ensures that you are giving the same general presentation each time. This lets you uncover any flaws or areas where improvement is needed. Drawing pictures on a note pad also works well.

Use your pen to highlight each point during the presentation.

Use Power Words. Yale University did a study and found that these were the 12 most persuasive words in the English language:

Easy	Results	Save
Discover	Guarantee	Safety
Health	Love	Money
Need	Proven	You

Key #5 Tell Stories To Make Points Clear

There are three reasons why successful salespeople use stories in their presentations:

- People enjoy stories. A good story is entertaining, informative and instructive.

- Stories put the imagination to work. Stories allow the merchant to engage their own representational system. It allows them to turn your words into pictures, sounds and feelings within their own mind.

- Stories can be used anywhere in the presentation. A good story can get your presentation back on track, emphasize a strong point, strengthen rapport, be used as a closing tool and much, much more.

The best stories are the ones that illustrate the benefits that other merchants have received from using your specific equipment or service. It's not always what you say but how you say it.

Here is one I've (Marc B) used several times when selling debit services. The customer is an auto repair shop using an old tranz 330 with no printer, and feels he doesn't need to upgrade his equipment.

"I have a customer just like you over at Midwest Tire Repair, What we did was upgrade him to a new machine so he could take debit and check cards. I'm sure you have seen all the advertisements on T.V. about check cards. You've probably got one in your wallet from your bank. Well up to 30% of all the credit cards you are taking are more than likely check cards, sometimes more (have backup article or material). You see when you process a check card through the terminal you have to pay the full discount rate like a credit card, but when you process the check card through your terminal using the pin pad you only pay a small flat transaction fee. Midwest's average ticket was $400.00 he was paying $7.05 per sale, with his new system he only pays .50 per check card regardless of the ticket amount. So if he does a $1,000 sale on a check card processed as a debit transaction he only pays .50 for that sale. It saved him enough to pay for all his new equipment. Not only that, but now when customers start to write a check he asks if they want to use their debit card. It cut his bad check losses in half, eliminated hand writing receipts and saved his office manager a trip to the bank." (Use simple straightforward language)

©Performance Training Systems

Make sure you have several true stories you can share with your customers about the benefits of your products offering. You may also want to discuss future technologies and how it is going to affect their business. Your stories should demonstrate how you remove pain from their current or future situation and add benefit.

Again, remember the golden rule. Answer this question for them.

WIIFM = What's in it for ME

Key #6 KISS – Keep it Short and Simple

Small business owners and corporate managers have limited time. Make sure you let them know that you appreciate the time given you and that it will be used wisely.

Remember is marketing to new businesses know very little about transaction processing speak in simple terms. Don't use industry jargon that will confuse and frustrate them.

Before we get into preventing objections lets take a look at why people buy.

▶ Chapter Thirty Six ◀

Why Do People Buy?

> *"The art of life is the art of avoiding pain; and he is the best pilot, who steers clearest of the rocks and shoals with which it is beset."*
> *- Thomas Jefferson*

The reason people buy is simple. *People buy for their own reasons, not yours!* Until you discover their dominant buying motive you won't know why they buy. Realize that their buying motives are influenced by two powerful forces driving their decision making process.

- **The Need to Avoid Pain or Fear of Loss**
  (Moving away motivation)

OR

- **The Need to Gain Pleasure or Benefit**
  (Moving toward motivation)

These two forces not only guide buying decisions but life decisions as well. Buying decisions are emotional. It takes a stronger emotion to overcome a weaker emotion. The only way to overcome the fear of pain is to make the desire for gain, or to be better off more intense.

These emotions can be experienced in the context of several time frames.

Pain or Pleasure in the present

"How many sales are you missing as we speak?"

©Performance Training Systems

"You could start making money today by accepting credit cards"

Pain or Pleasure in the future

"At this rate how much in lost sales will you have over the next 3 months"?

"Just think by this time next year you would not have had to worry about a single bad check"

Pain or Pleasure in the past

"How would you like to never have to worry about turning away a credit card sale again?"

"How would you like to reach the sales levels you had in the past by offering our loyalty program?"

The most powerful emotions are linked to the present. Show them how you can help today and/or avoid fear of loss today and you will get the sale.

The majority of people will do more to avoid pain than they will to gain pleasure. In fact studies have shown that pain is a 2.5 times greater motivator than pleasure. These behaviors are genetically and culturally programmed. Think about it, how did your parents motivate you as a child? Usually we are threatened with some type of consequence (spanking, grounding, lost privileges). A very small number of parents use pleasure or rewards to motivate their children.

When do most people make a major life change or modify their behavior? When the pain gets to great. Sit down one night and watch the majority of TV commercials and you will see they are using pain to motivate buyers. Do any of these ring a bell?

"Are you experience gas or bloating?"
"Can't cure that achy head cold?"
"Were moving them out fast, don't wait they won't last long"
"Mortgage rates won't stay this low much longer, refinance today"

It goes on and on.

This is simple psychology; often the most profound insights are simple. Just make sure you not only show your customer how much your products will benefit them, but how they will also alleviate their pain today.

If you would like to explore this idea further complete the exercise in Appendix E.

► Chapter Thirty Seven ◄
Preventing Objections

> *"Take your life in your own hands and what happens? A terrible thing: no one is to blame."*
> - Erica Jong

The best way to handle objections or roadblocks is to prevent them ahead of time. The extraordinary salesperson weaves the answers to the most common objections throughout their presentation.

When a merchant raises an objection one of the following is happening:

- **They Have Questions**
  "I need more information"

- **Defensive Reaction**
  "I feel threatened; fear or risk"

- **Emotional**
  "I am in a bad state"

- **They Need Help**
  "Help me make the right decision"

Here are the 7 steps that can help prevent objections:

1. Identify every conceivable objection. Most objections are pretty much the same regardless of what you sell.

2. Write them down.

3. Write down the answer to each objection and how to overcome it. (Prove it, put together visual aids, testimonials, articles, letters of reference etc.) Work with other salespeople in your office to brainstorm ideas.

4. Practice. Practice. Practice. Role-play with people.

5. Test in the field.

6. Make any revisions or changes.

7. Practice. Practice. Practice.

Complete the exercise in Appendix F to help prevent the most common objections.

► Chapter Thirty Eight ◄

"Great spirits have always encountered violent opposition from mediocre minds."
-Albert Einstein

What Benefits Do You Offer?

Before we can work on converting objections lets do a short exercise on the benefits your products and services.

List 10 things about your product or service that benefits your merchant the most: (What's in it for THEM)

1. _____
2. _____
3. _____
4. _____
5. _____
6. _____
7. _____
8. _____
9. _____
10. _____

List 5 things about your processor, ISO or bank that benefits your merchant the most:

1. _____

2. _____

3. _____

4. _____

5. _____

List 5 benefits of the equipment you are recommending to your merchant:

1. _____

2. _____

3. _____

4. _____

5. _____

List 5 things about you that ads value to your merchant:

1. _____

2. _____

3. _____

4. _____

5. _____

Now, that you know what benefits you bring to the table be ready to prove it. You must have visuals, articles and material that substantiates your claims without them it is all just talk.

▶ Chapter Thirty Nine ◀

Gaining Commitment

> *"People are always blaming their circumstances for what they are. I don't believe in circumstances. The people who get on in the world are the people who get up and look for the circumstances they want, and if they can't find them, make them."*
>
> *- George Bernard Shaw*

A great definition of gaining commitment is helping people make an educated buying decision. You've heard it before: "People don't like to be sold, but they love to buy." Your job is to create an environment where merchants want to buy. Lets look at the most common reason why prospects don't buy.

- **Fear of making a bad decision**
- **No perceived need and/or value**
- **They don't have the means to purchase**
- **Comfortable with current situation**
- **Lack of rapport or trust with sales person**
- **Had a previous negative experience**

The job of the merchant focused salesperson is to create a win-win situation with every customer, period. By now you should have the responses for your most common objections and how to master them. One thing to remember is that merchants want and need our services or you wouldn't be there.

Also keep in mind that many initial objections are conditioned responses, which means they are automatic. When someone in a retail store asks you "May I help you?"

how do you respond? Probably with "no thank you I'm just looking." Many of your merchants are doing the same thing.

Remember, people buy for their own reasons. Objections give you a good idea about what is really going on in their mind and the chance to re-verify what is really of true value to them.

Answering questions to objections should not be adversarial it is an opportunity to consummate the sale. Don't get defensive; an objection is not a personal attack.

Here are five traditional steps to overcoming objections:

1. Listen to the objection. Really listen.

2. Acknowledge the objection. Empathize and/or feed it back to them or ask a question to clarify the objection.

3. Answer the objection. It must be believable and practical to the situation. Use your prove it tools.

4. Confirm. Verify that the answer you gave is acceptable.

5. Advance the sale.

Traditional Closing Techniques

Many traditional closing techniques still work. If you have rapport, offered a solution that met the dominant buying motive and presented your product well, this step should be a natural progression.

©Performance Training Systems

The Alternate Choice

This is a technique where the client is given several options to choose from, usually just two. Regardless of the answer it will result in a sale.

- Would you like to start with the unit with the pin pad for $59.00 per month or the basic unit for $49.00 per month?
- Do you prefer delivery on Tuesday or Wednesday?
- Do you prefer the 48-month term or the 36-month term?
- Mr. Merchant, we have two programs. Program A is a lease to own for $39.95 for 48 months or Program B is our cash program for $995.00 cash, which do you prefer?
- Mr. Merchant we have two programs. Our platinum business development program offers you check imaging, gift cards, debit and credit for $89.95 per month or our silver program, which is debit, and credit only for $49.95 per month, which works best for you?

The list is endless. Multiple alternate choice closes can be created based on your individual product offering.

The Assumptive Close

This close assumes the merchant wants your equipment and services; you simply act by asking a question, then just start filling out the application. And why not, after the fantastic enthusiastic presentation you just gave!
Sample Questions:

- What is the legal name of your business?
- Do you have a copy of your business license handy?
- What is your tax id number?
- When did you want me to train your employees?
- Then I can assume we can move forward?

As long as the merchant continues to answer the questions, continue to assume that they have bought and finish your paperwork.

Feel, Felt, Found Method

This is a great close. It works with just about any objection raised.

The feel, felt, found method accomplishes three things:

- **Assures the merchant their feelings have been accepted**
- **Lets the merchant know those feelings are valid and shared by other merchants**
- **Shows the merchant that others have found those feelings to be unfounded because of one or more of the benefits of ownership**

I understand how you feel; I've had customers that felt the same way but what they found was that _____.

The Summation Close

The summation or recap close does exactly what it sounds like. It is a quick summation of all the benefits stated during the presentation that the merchant responded to.

"Mr. Merchant, just to summarize, the following benefits were important to you…"

1. That our new terminal will take all the major credit cards and the new smart cards being introduced to the market place, right?
2. One of the most important benefits we discussed was the ability to accept debit cards at a 0% discount fee and only a small transaction fee, right?
3. The new terminal is more user friendly than your current system and will decrease your checkout time, which will really help you in the Christmas rush, correct?
4. That we can set you up with our new gift card program to help increase cash flow immediately.

"Well, Mr. Merchant, considering everything, why don't we go ahead with the program? Or considering everything is there anything that would prevent us from moving forward?

Quit here and wait for a response. If positive, proceed, if negative, clarify the objection and advance the sale.

The Think It Over Close

This is one of the most common objections. This is the prospect that never makes a snap decision. He wants to sleep on it. When you hear, "I want to think it over," respond with:

Example:

That's fine, I understand. This is an important decision and you do need to feel comfortable with it. I know you want to make sure you covered all the bases. But, just to clarify my thinking and answer any questions you might have while I'm here, what is it that you want to think over? Is there something I didn't cover or is it the _____ or_____. (Keep firing possibilities at them in order to find out the true objection, i.e. is it the equipment? Is it the lease term? Is it our bank? Is it the price?)

The price should be mentioned last because it is the most common reason. This process will uncover the true objection. Once the true objection is uncovered you can deal with it.

Special Offer Close

Everybody wants a special deal; they want to feel they are getting the best value for their money. The only thing that limits a special offer is your imagination. Many times by building value in your sales presentation and by offering something the competition isn't you can hold your price.

Put a time limit on special offers. You want to create a sense of urgency.

Here are a few samples:

     Mr. Merchant for setting up with us today we are waiving the normal application fee of $95.00, and charging no installation fee.

     As an incentive Mr. Merchant we are currently offering five years free supplies for all new merchant that signup this month.

     As a bonus Mr. Merchant we are setting up all our customers up with a free 3-page website.

Mr. Merchant we have partnered with a local web design company and have arranged a special package for our customers. We can now offer you a custom 5 page website for only $99.00 this is a 60%.

Just for doing business with us today, Mr. Merchant we are including three valuable reports "How To Avoid Fraud" "How to Write a Business Plan" "How to Keep Gain Customer Loyalty".

Mr. Merchant we have partnered with XYZ communications and just for doing business with us today we are including a free cell phone and activation.

Mr. Merchant, we are currently giving all our new clients a free 1 hour consultation with a local accounting firm that we have partnered with, they can assist you will setting up your books and payroll system.

Mr. Merchant we are currently offering a free small business accounting system called quick books for our next 50 customers.

Use common sense. You can partner with many vendors wanting to reach this business market and often they will give you free product to giveaway.

When All Else Fails Just Ask Why?

Here is one technique that works in almost any situation and avoids using any pre-packed closing responses. Just ask the customer "Why." You can phrase this in many different ways here are a few:

Why do you say that?
I'm curious, why do you feel that way?
Tell me, why do you think that?

Why do you think my price is too high?
Why is that?

This will get down to the real objection very rapidly and you can work with the customer to eliminate their concerns.

► Chapter Forty ◄

Lets Talk About Price

Most salespeople make price a bigger issue than the customer does. Is price important? Of course it is. But very few people buy on price alone. If people bought on price alone they would be watching black and white TV's, driving compact cars, wearing nothing but timex watches and dressing in second hand clothes.

There are dozens of factors that influence a customers buying decisions, price is just one of them. In order to overcome a price issue your customer must believe that value out weighs price.

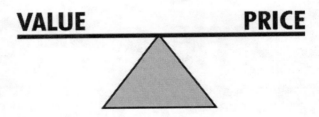

In order to tip the scales in your favor you must have an in-depth knowledge of the benefits you offer your merchant. You must emphasize your unique qualities and differentiate yourself from the competition.

Your terminal and rates may be the same as the next guy, but your total offer may be completely different. You may have key differences in several areas. See where you are better or different from your competitor and you will distinguish uniqueness in your offering.

Lets do an exercise, get a piece of paper out and create a column for each category and review your unique features and benefits (you may have multiple answers for each category):

For instance you may have the category company and one of your unique features is that you provide local customer service and have been in business in this area for over 10 years.

Category

Your Company

- Size (small or large can be a benefit)
- Credibility
- Awards
- Locality
- Time in Business
- Breadth of Products
- One Stop Shopping
- References
- Special Partners or Alliances
- Specific Expertise

Salesperson

- Years in the Business
- Life Experience
- Special Training
- Specific Expertise in Certain Niche
- Testimonials
- References
- Credibility

Banks or Vendors

    Clients They Service Now
    Funds Transfer
    Custom Programs (tips, car rental etc.)
    Size
    Credibility
    Awards
    Locality
    Time in Business
    Breadth of Products
    One Stop Shopping
    Specialize in Certain Types of Customers
    Reporting Capabilities
    Online products or services

Payment Terms

    Free Trial Period
    Leasing
    Special Terms (i.e. 3 payments same as cash)
    No Money Down
    Rental Program
    Accept Credit Cards

Special Offers

    Free Loaner Program
    Free Supplies
    Free Bonus Offering
    No Down Payment
    No Application Fee
    Free Reports
    Free Consultation
    Referral Fee
    Free Website
    Free Training

Rates and Fee

- Discount Rates
- Mid & Non-Qualified Rates
- Annual Fees
- Cancellation Fees
- Minimums
- Statement Fees
- Chargeback Fees
- Investigation Fees
- Batch Header Fees
- Investigation Fees
- Retrieval Fees
- Transaction Fees
- Application Fees

Equipment

- Warranty
- Ease of Use
- Training
- Delivery
- Special Payment Terms
- Future Capabilities
- Current Capabilities
- Upgrade Path
- Size of unit

Customer Service

- Hours of Operations
- Average hold time
- Size of Staff
- Awards
- Services Offered

Training

    Certification
    Type of Training
    Ongoing Training
    Personal or Phone
    No Charge

Installation

    Time Frame (how quick can the get it)
    Shipment
    Special Features About Installation
    Personal Installation

Now that you have the ammunition to create value for your merchant and overcome the competition. Choose 3-4 majors benefits in each category and be ready to use them in the sales process.

The sales professional must make the necessary changes to be successful in today's fast paced market. By combining the traditional closing techniques with new technologies, you will create a system that will yield consistently higher closing ratios.

The basics still apply! Sell yourself, your program and then ask for the business. Selling is fun - enjoy it, be good to your profession and it will be good to you!

©Performance Training Systems

► Chapter Forty One ◄

Follow Up

> *"We are what we repeatedly do.* ***Excellence, then, is not an act, but a habit."***
> — *Aristotle*

Okay you did everything you could but didn't make the sale. Now you have to follow-up, this is where the money is. Make sure before leaving the merchant a follow-up time and date has been set.

This is where 90% of salespeople drop the ball. If you left the appointment and agreed to call him next Tuesday at 2:00, then call him next Tuesday at 2:00. You will impress him with your ability to follow up on your commitments.

Make sure you maintain a database (Outlook, Act or Goldmine are good choices) or paper follow-up system.

Here are some pointers to help close follow-up sales:

- **Send them a thank you note.**
- **Fax or email them an industry related article. (i.e. smart card implementation, fraud, or debit related)**
- **Call with a special limited time offer to close the sale.**
- **Send an e-card.**
- **Refer a customer to their company.**
- **Put them in your auto responder follow up system.**
- **Put them on your newsletter list.**

► Chapter Forty Two ◄

Time Management

"Time is life. It is irreversible and irreplaceable. To waste your time is to waste your life, but to master your time is to master you life and make the most of it."
-Alan Lakein

Here are some interesting facts to consider:

- There are only 86,400 seconds or 1440 minutes or 24 hours in our day – period. How this time is utilized will determine your success or failure in this life.

- The average person today receives more information on a daily basis than the average person received in a lifetime in 1900.

- Between 1900 and 1998 life expectancy in the United States increased from 51 to 80 for females and 48 to 74 for males.

- The life expectancy for females born in the year 2050 is 87 years and for males it is 81 years.

- The average males heart will beat 2,791,743,120 times during his lifetime and he will take 581,613,150 breaths of air.

- The average human being has roughly 60,000 thoughts a day.

- The average person spends less than two minutes per day in meaningful communication with their spouse or "significant other".

- 28% of all households have two TVs, 28% of all households have three TVs, 20% of all households have four TVs, and 12% of all households have five or more TVs.

- On an average day 31% of all children will watch 1-3 hours of TV, 17% will watch more than 5 hours a day.

- 75% of heart attacks occur between the hours of 5:00am – 8:00am.

- More heart attacks occur on Monday than on any other day of the week.

- 80% of people do not want to go to work on Monday. That number drops to 60% by Friday.

- There are 17 Million meetings per day in America.

- The average person gets 6 hours and 57 minutes of sleep per night.

- The average person spends 35 minutes per day commuting.

- 1 hour of planning will save you 10 hours of doing.

Pareto's Law

Almost 100 years ago Vilfredo Pareto, an Italian economist, conducted a study on income and wealth patterns. He discovered a "predictable imbalance" that shows up in every area of life. This is now known as the Pareto Time Principle, or the 80/20 Rule. The 80/20 rule means that 80% of time spent poorly produces 20% of desired results, while 20% of time spent wisely nets 80% of the desired results.

Examples of the Pareto principle include:

80% of the sales a salesperson makes come from 20% of their cold calls.

20% of the automobiles on the road cause 80% of the accidents.

20% of the producers create 80% of the production volume.

80% of the useful information on the Internet comes from 20% of the sites.

80% of what makes you happy comes from 20% of the people with whom you are close.

One of the secrets of success is to stay focused on the 20% of our lives that will help us reach our goals and mission. By devoting more time and effort on the 20% that matters, you gain tremendous leverage in your life.

Every 1% improvement in effectiveness produces five percent more in desired results! That's the power of Pareto's Law.

▶ Chapter Forty Three ◀

What's Your Time Worth?

"One thing you can't recycle is wasted time."
-Anon

We all know we don't have enough hours in the day to do the things we want to accomplish. You've heard it before "Time is Money". But just how much is your time worth?

There are roughly 1,952 working hours in a year of 244 working days. This assumes you don't work Saturdays, which I would recommend doing at least once a month.

Earning Per Year	Value of an Hour
$30,000	$15.35
$40,000	$20.50
$50,000	$25.60
$60,000	$30.73
$70,000	$35.86
$80,000	$40.98
$90,000	$46.10
$100,000	$51.22

Now that you see how much each hour of your time is worth you can understand the importance of time management. The most profitable hours are those that you spend in front of a qualified merchant.

If dedicated to being a professional, how efficiently you allocate your assets (your time, your skills, your resources) determines your ability to deliver results to your customers.

©Performance Training Systems

We all start with the same 24 hours every day. Why do some people seem to effortlessly get their work done in the same amount of time while others struggle? The successful salesperson has learned how to manage assets around time. You always want the maximum ROT (Return on your Time.)

Successful people utilized their time to its fullest by ensuring all their actions are targeted toward those things that mean the most, with their individual goals and mission.

There are many great time management tools in the marketplace, select something that fits your personal style. If you work on computers get a software-based system like Act, Goldmine or Outlook.

I recommend a software-based solution this will allow you to create a database of your customers and continually keep in touch with them on a periodic basis.

Remember, time is a finite resource – use it wisely.

> *"First I was dying to finish high school and to start college. And then I was dying for my children to grow old enough for school, so I could return to work. And then I was dying to retire. And now I am dying and suddenly realized I forgot to live"*
> *- Source Unknown*

©Performance Training Systems

▶ Chapter Forty Four ◀

Tips on Organizing Your Time

> *"Far better to dare mighty things, to win glorious triumphs, even though checkered by failure, than to take rank with those poor spirits who neither enjoy much nor suffer much, because they live in the gray twilight that knows not victory, nor defeat."*
> – Theodore Roosevelt

Develop a Daily Routine:

- **Review your Goals and Mission statement every morning before work**
- **Get started early**
- **Review your to-do list for the day and work your way down from the highest priority to the lowest priority**
- **Read or listen to a personal growth or motivational program daily**
- **Use the Daily Call Sheet in the Appendix**

The Sales Hours:

Organize your time around the sales hours- the hours that you can be talking to prospects and customers.

Perform all non-revenue generating activities before or after your sales hours.

Prospecting Hours:

Dedicate a certain percentage of sales hours to prospecting. Vary your time for prospecting and see what yields the best results.

Track your calls and results so you can create a sales formula for success.

Follow Up:

Create templates for your follow letters and correspondence for easy distribution.

Perform your follow up everyday; this is where the money is!

Professional Development:

Continue sharpening your saw as Stephen Covey puts it; attend training at least 4 times per year.

Schedule exercise and personal growth during non-sales hours.

Listen to audiotapes while you're in the car. Create a rolling audio library to enhance your skills.

► Chapter Forty Five ◄

Goal Setting

> *"A vision without a task is but a dream; a task without a vision is drudgery; a vision and a task is the hope of the world."*
> — *Church in Sussex, England*

Why does almost every book on self-improvement speak about goals? Because goal-setting works. If you don't know where and more importantly **WHY** you're moving in a particular direction, you'll never arrive at that destination.

A long-term study conducted in 1953 of graduates of Yale University demonstrates my point. The graduates were asked if they had written goals for their future and what they want to accomplish.

Only 3% had written goals. In 1973, the researches interviewed the graduates again. They discovered that the 3% that had specific written goals were worth more financially, happier, more fulfilled than the entire group of 97% that did not have written goals.

According to a study done by several well know doctors – goals are more likely to improve performance when three conditions are met.

1. The Goal must be SPECIFIC.

Defining a goal as doing the best you can is as bad as having no goal at all. You need to be specific about what you are going to do and by when you are going to do it.

2. The Goal must be CHALLENGING but ACHIEVABLE.

You will work harder for tough but realistic goals than for easy goals that pose no challenge or impossible goals that can never be attained.

3. The Goal should be framed in the terms of GETTING WHAT YOU WANT RATHER THAN AVOIDING WHAT YOU DO NOT WANT.

Approach Goals are positive experiences that you seek directly. Avoidance Goals are unpleasant experiences that you hope to avoid. People that frame their goals in Approach terms have much better results in accomplishing their goals.

Here is an acronym that helps me. Make sure you create:

SMART Goals:

Specific	Identify exactly what you want
Measurable	Quantify your outcome: how much, how big, what size, etc. –when will you know you accomplished your goal
Action	Plan the work - Work the plan
Realistic	The goal is within your realm of possibility
Time Specific	When will the goal be accomplished?

NOTE: You must ensure that your goals are aligned with your values and they support your life mission.

If you are ready to work on a life plan go to our website and download the Life Design Workshop for free at www.bankcard101.com.

In this workshop you will develop a legacy statement, mission statement, determine your core values, and develop goals in the following areas:

- **Personal Development**
- **Career**
- **Financial**
- **Material**
- **Spiritual**
- **Health**
- **Family/Relationships**

Once you have completed the Life Design Workshop you will know what you stand for and where you are going.

DO IT NOW!

▶ Chapter Forty Six ◀

Motivation 101

> *"People often say that Motivation doesn't last. Well, neither does bathing. That's why we recommend it daily."*
> *-Zig Ziglar*

The word motivation, like the word emotion, comes from the Latin root meaning "to move," and the psychology of motivation is indeed the study of what moves us, why we do what we do. For our purposes, motivation will refer to any process that causes a person to move toward a goal or away from an unpleasant situation.

Remember the two controlling factors in our lives:

- **The Need To Avoid Pain**
  Away From Motivation

  OR

- **The Desire To Gain Pleasure**
  Toward Motivation

These motivation strategies are nothing new; Aristotle observed this phenomenon thousands of years ago. The majority of people will react out of fear of loss more than the desire for gain.

Let's look at an example:

The alarm goes off in the morning, you think to yourself "It's morning already, I'll sleep a few more minutes" and hit the snooze button? 10 minutes later the alarm goes off, an inner voice says "It's time to get up?" your mind might show you pictures of yourself rushing to get ready and missing breakfast. But the bed is soooo warm, and you think, "No big deal, I'll skip breakfast" so you hit the snooze again.

A few minutes later the alarm goes off again. This time your inner voice says, "You've got to get up, you're going to be late and really get in trouble." This time your mind starts showing you pictures of being late and having to explain it to your sales manager. But you think, "I can drive a little faster and still make it." So back to sleep you go.

This time the little voice in your head screams, "GET UP, GET UP, YOU'VE GOT TO GET UP, YOU ARE DEAD MEAT" This time your brain starts showing you pictures of getting to office late, missing the sales meeting, having your sales manager screaming at you and losing your job. Now that the picture is bright and clear you motivated yourself by making up scenarios of what you want to move **AWAY FROM**.

Let's look at one more example:

Have you ever been on vacation, maybe at a nice resort or hotel and as you opened your eyes, you began to visualize what you and your family were going to do for the day? You pictured all the great stuff that was available and it pulled you out of bed like a magnet. The question was, what would I do first? Not whether to get up or not. This is an example of moving **TOWARD** motivation.

We have all developed a motivation strategy. We become more motivated by either moving toward images of success, pleasure, and achievement or away from failure, pain and loss.

Determine your motivation style, neither is better or worse. The key is learning to use your particular strategy to your advantage.

Motivation is also affected by your expectations, values and beliefs. How hard you will work for something often depends on your desire and what you expect to accomplish – your goals. If you are confident of success, you will often work harder to achieve your goals.

Once again, a value is a central motivating belief, reflecting a person's fundamental beliefs and ideals: freedom, independence, beauty, equality, friendship, fun, adventure, fame, wisdom, peace, acceptance and so on.

Your attitude is a key factor in creating success and staying motivated. We have all been down roads that were dead ends. With a winning attitude, you can handle set backs, see it for what it is, a learning experience, and move on to the next challenge.

Remember, you have the power to choose your attitude on a daily basis. Choosing a positive attitude is choosing to be successful.

The greatest plan in the world will not be executed without hard work. I once went to a seminar and each seat contained a piece of paper with the phrase "The Secret To Becoming A Millionaire." When the speaker came out he invited us to open the piece of paper to learn the secret. The note simply said "Hard Work."

Motivation is a tool to move us to action. Without action we cannot accomplish our goals in life. Few things that are worthwhile come easy. Hard work is a key ingredient to staying motivated and accomplishing your dreams.

Self-Motivation is the key factor is creating what you want in your life. With motivation you will have the required persistence to be successful.

Interview With David J. Bartone, Esq.

David J. Bartone is a Washington, D.C. and California based attorney whose practice areas include litigation and business transactions in credit and debit card processing, electronic commerce, banking, mortgage and finance law, securities regulation and white collar crime. Mr. Bartone has represented clients before all courts and the federal government regulatory agencies. His representation of clients in electronic commerce has focused on numerous federal and state issues prevalent today within the credit card and ATM industries. Mr. Bartone has extensive experience in litigating disputes involving credit card and ATM portfolios. Mr. Bartone also offers general business and legal consultation to clients involved in electronic commerce, including consultation relating to federal and state regulation affecting electronic commerce and purchase and sale of credit card and ATM portfolios.

Mr. Bartone received his Juris Doctor from the Catholic University of America in 1985. He served as law clerk to the Honorable Nicholas S. Nunzio in Washington, D.C. from 1985-1986. He is the author of "The ATM Surcharge Dispute in California: What Happens in the Wake of Judge Walker's Preliminary Ruling in Favor of National Banks," Article, Kiosk Magazine, February 2001. Mr. Bartone is Rated "AV" by the Martindale-Hubbell Law Directory and is a Member of the Martindale-Hubbell Bar Register of Preeminent Lawyers, 2002. He is also a Member of The National Registry of Who's Who, 1999.

Question: What do you feel are the major legal issues facing the credit card processing industry at this time?

©Performance Training Systems

DB: The Electronic Signatures Act. On June 30, 2000, President Clinton signed the Electronic Signatures in Global and National Commerce Act (the "Electronic Signatures Act" or the "Act"). The Electronic Signatures Act took effect on October 1, 2000. The Act is designed to facilitate the use of electronic records and signatures in interstate or foreign commerce. The Act affords electronic signatures and electronic documents legal status equivalent to that of traditional handwritten signatures and paper documents.

The Act does not require that a person agree to use or accept electronic records or electronic signatures. Instead, it grants the freedom to individuals and businesses to choose whether they want to receive and execute documents electronically. Among other things, the Act provides that if a statute or regulation requires that information relating to a transaction in interstate commerce be provided to a consumer in writing, the use of an electronic record to provide the information satisfies the "writing" requirement if the consumer consent requirements of the Electronic Signatures Act are met.

Question: How will this impact our industry?

DB: The Electronic Signatures Act has had, and will continue to have, a substantial impact on the credit card processing industry given the explosion of e-commerce and the use of credit cards in e-commerce.

Most businesses can take advantage of the law since the Act applies to "any transaction in or affecting interstate or foreign commerce." It should be noted, however, that ink and paper are still required: for the creation and execution of wills, codicils and testamentary trusts; to adopt, divorce or resolve other matters of family law; to provide notice of cancellation or termination of utility services or the default, acceleration, repossession, foreclosure or eviction under a credit agreement secured by the primary residence of an individual; the cancellation or termination of health or life insurance benefits; the recall of a product or notification of a failure of a product; and any document required to accompany the transportation of handling of hazardous or other dangerous materials.

The Act contains complex provisions, which govern its application to consumer transactions. Perhaps the most significant benefit of the Act is in connection with document retention. According to the new legislation, a business can comply with statutory and regulatory retention requirements by storing the record or contract electronically. With respect to this latter point, businesses are still required to retain their records for the period required by statute. The Act does permit federal and state regulatory agencies to still require the retention of paper documents.

Since the Electronic Signatures Act was signed into law, numerous states have adopted the Uniform Electronics Transactions Act ("UETA"). Like the Electronic Signatures Act, the UETA provides that a record or signature may not be denied legal effect or enforceability solely because it is in an electronic form. However, the Electronic Signatures Act contains more restrictions on the use of electronic signatures and electronic documents. While the two statutes both regulate the same area, the Electronic Signatures Act generally will control to the extent there is a conflict between the federal and state laws.

The Electronic Signature Act seems to make good sense. A legal signature is the mark of a specific individual against a specific document at a specific time given with specific intent. The act of providing a signature is a ceremonial process. It has been part of our culture for hundreds of years. The ceremony is important in demonstrating the signatory's legal undertaking of a particular action.

In general terms, where the law requires a signature, an e-signature satisfies the requirement, with the exception of execution of the various documents identified above. A computer record can be considered "hearsay" by some courts, including federal courts. If the record is considered hearsay, then the party seeking to introduce the record must make the record fall within an exception to the hearsay rule. Computer records are usually admitted into evidence under the business records exception to the hearsay rule.

An authenticity foundation must also be laid by the party producing the record as evidence. The key step to laying a foundation is authenticating the record. Authenticating an electronic computer record is no different than authenticating other records. Authenticating a record means evidence sufficient to support a finding that the matter in question is what its proponent claims. The other party in court would challenge the authenticity of computer records on one of three general grounds by challenging: (1) the storing and retention of the stored records, and whether they were changed, manipulated, or damaged after they were created; (2) the reliability of the computer program that stores and generates the computer records with particular regard to whether the system is reliable and whether it has flaws, programming errors or bugs; and, (3) the identity of the author, which requires an indicia of proof that the computer records really are connected to a particular person.

Question: How does that benefit our industry?

DB: **The benefits conferred upon the credit card processing industry and commercial and non-commercial entities engaged in e-commerce as a result of the implementation of electronic signatures is substantial. Electronic signatures can offer greater security, reliability and transparency in credit card processing by minimizing the risk of dealing with fraud, or persons who attempt to escape responsibility by claiming to have been impersonated. Electronic signatures can satisfy the need of message integrity by preventing unauthorized access to data, detecting any message tampering and diminishing the danger of false claims that data was changed after it was sent. Therefore open network systems can be made more efficient with data interchanges among businesses and cost-effective and safe information gathering respecting a consumer's right of online privacy. In addition, when an "e-contract" in credit card processing is electronically signed, the formal legal requirements (writing, originality of signature and of document) are satisfied, since digital signatures are functionally equivalent to paper forms.**

Question: What do you think the future looks like in the industry?

DB: **I see continued migration to a cashless society, for years; analysts have predicted the elimination of physical cash as a transaction medium. Such a transaction medium has been referred to as a "cashless society." Substituted in the place of cash would be an electronic payment system, in one form or**

another. Some analysts look at such a prospect optimistically, believing that a cashless society would increase the efficiency of the economy. Still, others, view such a prospect pessimistically believing that it would subject the most private details of our lives to scrutiny and publication. Whatever the outcome, such a radical transformation will undoubtedly have a substantial affect on the credit card processing industry.

Attention to the possibility of a cashless society has increased and intensified over the past several years. Those who are enthusiastic over the prospect of eliminating cash as a transaction medium believe that the immediate benefits would be profound and fundamental. Theft of cash would become impossible. Bank robberies and cash register robberies might cease to occur. Attacks on shopkeepers, taxi drivers, and cashiers could end. Urban streets might very well become safer. Security costs and insurance rates might possibly fall. Property values could very well rise. The sale of illegal drugs, along with related violent crime could diminish. Hospital emergency rooms might become less crowded. A change from cash to recorded electronic money might be accompanied by a flow of previously unpaid income tax revenues in the billions of dollars. As a result, income tax rates could be lowered or the national debt reduced.

Not all proponents are as ecstatic about the benefits of a cashless society. However, regardless of the advantages, or disadvantages, some observers think that it might only be a matter of time before the cashless society becomes a reality. Many describe the elimination of coins and currency any time soon as a myth.

Whatever the criticism, the elimination of cash transactions is fast becoming technically feasible. There need not be a unitary government-run electronic monetary system for cash to disappear. Many electronic and other non-cash payments means are already in use. Credit cards, debit cards, prepayment cards, and smart cards are established components of a non-cash transaction system. Checks, of course, are a non-cash payment means also, but do not fit either into the electronic cashless society visualized by its proponents.

Credit cards are in such widespread use so as to hardly require discussion. The credit card business has been characterized by some as being saturated. Not strictly a payment means, but a promise of deferred payment, credit cards nonetheless can substitute for the use of cash. Debit cards have been available for years. They represent a true payment means since the amount of the purchase is taken from an account belonging to the customer. Despite there being millions of debit cards in use, whether the relative volume of purchases made with them exceeds those of cash is debatable.

Question: What other products do you see impacting the marketplace?

DB: Use of debit cards seems likely to grow throughout the decade. Many were reluctant to issue them in the past because of technical problems and the perceived difficulty of making them profitable. However, both Visa and MasterCard launched campaigns to gain more extensive use of their debit cards. These campaigns encompass trying to sign up more banks as issuers and educating consumers in their use. They have also been seeking additional outlets, which have not traditionally taken credit cards, including taxicabs

©Performance Training Systems

and fast food outlets. Even welfare recipients are using a form of debit cards.

ATMs have facilitated the use of cash by making cash easily available at any time, just about anywhere. However, ATMs which dispense "scrip" spend able at the retailer in which the ATM is located have made a resurgence into the marketplace. Such scrip machines should appeal to retailers as another means of making it easy for customers to spend money while being much cheaper to have on site than an ATM. They are also less attractive to criminals than cash ATMs.

Prepayment cards store value on magnetic, electronic, or optical media, often in appearance much like a credit card. When used, the accepting device erases the proper portion of the value. Prepayment cards have had substantial use overseas, and their use in the United States has grown substantially over the past few years. Smart cards are in a sense an extension of the prepayment cards. Like the prepayment cards, they can store value for future use, but they also include an internal microchip based processing capability. Smart cards have been little used in the United States, but are common in Europe.

Economic hurdles may limit the development of alternative systems, which are technically feasible. The cost of paper handling and getting authorizations accompanying the acceptance of credit and debit cards has been a barrier in the past, especially for moderate size transactions. The development of low cost point of sale terminals has been eliminating the need for this paper handling since it makes possible the exclusively electronic handling of the transaction. This has resulted in a substantial reduction in the cost of an average credit authorization over the past several years. The cost of handling transactions electronically is approaching the level that makes even relatively small purchases with electronic payment means feasible. Such non-paper exchanges can now have a cost advantage over checks.

Lack of consumer acceptance has impeded the spread of debit cards and may also slow further advances in electronic payments means. The problem may partly have been the name "debit card." To combat this, such cards are often referred to as cash or check cards. Another obstacle is that for many consumers there is no net advantage to debit cards. There is an element of convenience over carrying cash or even a checkbook. However, the user loses the deferred payment feature inherent in credit cards and assumes greater potential liability if the card is lost or stolen. Considering these factors, it might be fair to say that those who pay off their credit card balances every month will in most cases be better off with one of the many no-fee credit cards now available than with a debit card. Many consumers are likely to reach the same conclusion, though those who do not qualify for credit cards may find debit cards appealing. It appears that consumer's still use cash more than any other payment means for personal expenditures.

It is not merely drug dealers or other criminals who are concerned with the privacy afforded by cash transactions. Others are worried about the detailed record of their transactions left by non-cash transactions. Non-cash transactions substantially jeopardize privacy, which is lost with the current electronic credit, debit and smart cards. For example, it give the opportunity for strangers to accumulate and swap portfolios of information evidencing a number of things that most persons would care to remain private, including, but not limited to, what videos or games a person rents at the video store, what books are purchased in bookstores or what is otherwise purchased at any store or on the internet.

Further, cynics say they do not trust politicians who tell everyone that by snooping in merchants' databases they will succeed in protecting the privacy of consumers. Instead, they believe that the politicians will use the data for their own political purposes – collecting taxes, attempting to reduce national health care costs, getting re-elected, etc. Fear of being tracked in detail is not groundless. For example, card associations provide services that allow banks to more precisely analyze cardholders' buying patterns and target sales and promotions to customers. Prepayment cards are generally anonymous in use. However, there is no technological barrier to the issuer encoding information about the purchaser on the card and tracking its use. In addition, systems have point-of-use devices networked to computers to spot misuse of the cards. It is not hard to visualize the practice expanding.

The elimination of physical cash from our economy is already feasible from a purely technological perspective. The economic barriers are also disappearing, though a substantial additional investment in equipment and cards would be needed to permit the purchase of small-ticket items. Some mechanism to permit easy transfer from one person to another would also have to be provided. There do not seem to be adequate incentives to induce any entity or group of entities to make this substantial investment in the near-term. Thus, any transition to a cashless society is likely to be gradual.

An even greater obstacle to the elimination of physical cash is consumer resistance. In spite of the availability of a variety of non-cash payment means, there has not been a substantial decline in the relative use of cash over the past decade. Even among those consumers who are not concerned over the privacy implications, simple inertia requires a greater incentive for change than has so far been evident.

The cashless society, then, seems to be a far distant vision. It is only a few years closer to fulfillment than when first expounded many years ago.

Question: What trends do you see taking place that will affect our industry?

DB: As financial institutions search for more secure authentication methods for bankcard processing, e-commerce, computer user-access and other security applications, biometrics is gaining increasing attention in the business and legal communities. After years of research and development, several biometric identification systems have been developed. Some are relatively new, but even in their fledgling state, those systems have substantially improved the integrity of identification processes.

Security systems normally utilize three types of authentication methods: (1) something the user knows (a password, PIN, or piece of personal information (such as your mother's maiden name, for example); (2) something the user owns – a card key, smart card, or token, like a secure ID card; and/or, (3) something the user is; that is, a physical aspect of the person's being – a biometric. Of these, a biometric is the most secure and convenient authentication tool. It cannot be borrowed, stolen, or forgotten, and forging one is practically impossible. Biometrics measures an individual's unique physical and/or behavioral characteristics to recognize or authenticate that person's identity. Common physical biometrics include: fingerprints; hand or palm geometry; and retina, iris, or facial characteristics. Behavioral characters include signature, voice (which also has a physical component), keystroke pattern, and gait. Of this class of biometrics, the technology for signature and voice are the most developed.

A fingerprint looks at the patterns found on a fingertip. The thumbprint is commonly used. There are a variety of approaches to fingerprint verification. Some emulate the traditional police method of matching the details of the print. Others use straight pattern-matching devices. Some verification approaches can detect when a *live* finger is presented and when it is not. A greater variety of fingerprint devices are available than for any other biometric. As the price of these devices and processing costs decreases, using fingerprints for identification purposes is gaining acceptance, despite the common-criminal stigma.

Hand geometry involves analyzing and measuring the shape of the hand. This biometric offers a good balance of performance characteristics and is relatively easy to use. It might be suitable where there are more users or where users access the system infrequently and are perhaps less disciplined in their approach to the system. Accuracy can be very high if desired, and flexible performance tuning and configuration can accommodate a wide range of applications. Organizations are using hand geometry readers in various scenarios, including time and attendance recording, where they have proven themselves to be extremely popular. Ease of integration into other systems and processes, coupled with ease of use, makes hand geometry an obvious first step for many biometric projects.

A retina-based biometric involves analyzing the layer of blood vessels situated at the back of the eye. It is an established technology that involves using a low-intensity light source through an optical coupler to scan the unique patterns of the retina. Retinal scanning can be quite accurate. However, the downside is that it requires the user to look into a receptacle and focus on a given point. This is not particularly convenient if the user wears glasses or is concerned about having close contact with the reading device. For these reasons, all users do not warmly accept retinal scanning, even though the technology itself is reported to work well.

An iris-based biometric, on the other hand, involves analyzing features found in the colored ring of tissue that surrounds the pupil. Iris scanning is undoubtedly the least intrusive of the eye-related biometrics because it uses a fairly conventional camera and requires no close contact between the user and the reader. In addition, it has the potential for higher than average matching performance. Iris biometrics work with glasses in place and is one of the few devices that can work well in identification mode. Ease of use and system integration have not traditionally been strong points with iris scanning devices, it is expected that improvements in these areas will be made as new products emerge.

Face recognition analyzes facial characteristics. It requires a digital camera to develop a facial image of the user for authentication. This technique has attracted considerable interest, although many people do not completely understand its capabilities. Some vendors have made extravagant claims, which are very difficult, if not impossible, to substantiate in practice, for facial recognition devices. Because facial scanning needs an extra peripheral not customarily included with basic computers, it is more of a niche market for network authentication. However, the casino industry has capitalized on this technology to create a facial database of scam artists for quick detection by security personnel.

Security systems use the aforesaid biometrics, among others, for two basic purposes. The first is to verify a user; the second is to identify a user. Identification tends to be the more difficult of the two uses because a system must search a database of enrolled users to find a match. The biometric that a security system employs depends in part on what the system is protecting and what it is trying to protect against.

E-commerce developers are exploring the use of biometrics, smart cards and bankcards to verify a party's identity more accurately. For example, many banks are interested in this combination to authenticate customers and ensure non-repudiation of online banking, trading, and purchasing transactions. Point-of-sales (POS) system vendors are working on the cardholder verification method, which would enlist smart cards and biometrics to replace signature verification and use of personal identification numbers. MasterCard has estimated that maintaining that adding smart-card-based biometric authentication to a POS credit card payment will decrease fraud by 80 percent. Some developers are using biometrics to obtain secure services over the telephone through voice authentication. Voice authentication systems are currently deployed nationwide. Some developers use the catch phrase: "No PIN to remember, no PIN to forget."

Accompanying the implementation of some of these systems, there has been an ongoing debate over two issues: (1) effectiveness and infringement on civil liberties; and, (2) the implementation of this type of software. Face recognition has been criticized as being a potential violation of our civil liberties. Privacy is a major concern, especially when the general public may be somewhat uninformed of the capabilities of such a system. On the flipside of this debate, many people feel that biometric technologies are imperative to the prevention of fraud in bankcard processing and e-commerce and our security in the wake of September 11. They also argue that it could be a great tool for apprehending criminals as well. Advocates in favor of such technology place emphasis on the fact that if you are obeying the law then you should not worry about the existence of this technology.

Interview With Bob Carr

Bob Carr is the Founder, CEO and Chairman of Heartland Payment Systems, the nation's largest privately owned merchant acquirer and ninth largest overall, with annual revenues exceeding $300,000,000. Heartland was recognized by INC Magazine as the 57th fastest-growing private company in America and is one of the 10 largest INC 500 companies. Bob was a Founder and Vice President from 1988 to '90 of the Bankcard Services Association, which has since become the ETA.

Before entering the bankcard industry in 1986, he developed computer software systems for unattended fuel pumps and created the first integrated accounting applications for PCs. He also started the computer department at the Bank of Illinois and served as the Director of the Computer Center and as a mathematics instructor for Parkland College. He earned degrees in mathematics and computer science from the University of Illinois in 1966 and 1967.

Question: What advice would you give to a new salesperson entering the industry?

BC: First, decide your objectives. Is your objective to make big bucks in the short term and get out or is your objective to establish a long-term career? If your objective is to establish a long-term career, then find a role model. Find someone who has done the same thing successfully for a few years with the same company(s). Decide the value proposition you are going to offer your merchants. Do the math. How many merchants do you think you can deliver on the great service you will be promising? How will you make a living while you are building your portfolio and deliver

what you promise all at the same time?

Question: In your opinion what are the critical characteristics that salespeople in this industry need to possess to be successful?

BC: Successful salespeople need to have the same characteristics as most other entrepreneurs. They need to be tenacious, self-motivated, thick-skinned and smart to make it long term in our industry. If the position is commission based add the following characteristics: self-confident, willing to work very long hours, willing to study and study the technical and business details of the industry and the competition and be willing to accept the risk of failure.

Question: Do you feel a salesperson entering in the industry now has the potential to earn a substantial income?

BC: These are the best of times and the worst of times. They are the best of times for people looking for a long-term career and willing to prepare for that career over months and years. It is the worst of times for people trying to make quick bucks by selling overpriced priced equipment with false promises of low rates. Merchants have already played that game and they have learned to hate it. If you can deliver true value to a large number of merchants with integrated products, a very bright future lays ahead.

Question: What do you think the future looks like for the industry?

BC: Our industry is in its adolescence. The future is extremely bright but the roadmap is hazy. Those who can conceive, develop, and sell value-added, integrated payment solutions are going to set the future direction of the payments industry. It will be fun to watch and take another 5-7 years to see a dominant direction.

Question: What challenges do you feel our industry is facing?

BC: Our industry must overcome the sins of the fast buck artists of the late 80s and 90s. In the old days, it was an honor to represent the bank card associations. Millions of merchants have been burned by companies and salespeople who abused the brands of Visa and MasterCard and they now look upon the industry's salespeople with automatic distrust.

A second challenge is the concentration of power into the hands of a few companies with a lot of power.

Question: What products do you see coming out that will impact the industry the most? i.e. – biometrics, smart cards, etc?

BC: Payroll processing, debit cards, integrated bank services such as deposit reconciliation, time and attendance, prepaid cards, electronic check truncation, smart cards and biometrics will all play major roles in the future of the payments industry.

Interview with Mary Dees

Mary F. Dees is a 22-year veteran of the financial services, payment product, credit card and transaction processing industries. Mary's background includes positions at major corporations and financial services companies. These include: CBS, Merrill Lynch, Barclays VISA travelers cheques, First Bank System/Rocky Mountain Bankcard, First USA Financial Services and Paymentech, Inc.

Mary is currently President & CEO of Creditranz.com, Inc., a Dallas based company providing services in the electronic transaction industry. During her career she has been an integral member of project teams that have introduced unique corporate, purchasing and fleet card issuing products, Internet transaction processing software and merchant card processing services. In 2002 and 2003, she served as a court appointed receiver and general manager for an Independent Sales Organization placed in a Federal Court receivership during an investigation by the FTC.

Mary's industry development activities have included a variety of positions on various boards and committees over the years. These include: President-Elect, Treasurer, Secretary and Director, Electronic Transactions Associations and Chairman, Industry Relations Committee; US and Global Corporate Products Advisory Committees, Merchant Advisory Committee, MasterCard International; Commercial Product Advisory Committee, VISA USA; and Chairman, Telemoney Advisory Committee.

Question: Do you feel a salesperson entering in the industry now has the potential to earn a substantial income?

MD: Yes. There are still tremendous

opportunities in this industry. Technology is always changing and evolving. The advent of alternative communications options and enhanced product features continues to bring new value to merchants and new ways for salespeople to differentiate their products and service.

Question: What advice would you give to a new salesperson entering the industry?

MD: Focus on your customer first and foremost. Perform thorough due diligence, understand your customer's needs and analyze how your products and services can help a specific customer to become more efficient, effective and successful.

Question: What tools do you think are most important for the field sales reps?

MD: The most important tool is a good education in the industry. Additionally, good reference materials that provide both a framework to assist the salesperson in presenting the program and also helping merchants understand the more complex elements of card processing.

Question: What do you think the future looks like for the industry?

MD: I think that the future remains strong for the transaction processing industry since our economy continues to become increasingly more reliant on electronic methods of facilitating commerce and the transfer of information.

Question: What challenges do you feel our industry faces?

MD: Our industry will continue to face consolidation due to the continued pressure on pricing, expense management and scale. The industry will also face increased scrutiny and government intervention relative to the practices, pricing and products in the small merchant market.

Question: What products do you see coming out that will impact the industry the most?

MD: I think smart cards will have a significant impact on the industry. It will introduce new features and functionality available for both consumers and merchants and will require a massive change in the technology currently deployed in the market. Since there is not a current standard for smart cards in the US that must be established and then the devices will either need to be upgraded or replaced based on that standard. I think that biometrics for general-purpose retail will be a longer-term introduction. The concept of biometrics for the purchases of airline tickets at the airport has a very legitimate application now in the current situation of national security and the fight against terrorism. I don't think that we have evolved to a point where a consumer would be interested in having their fingerprint on file to purchase an article of clothing. I think if we have increased concerns on fraud, money laundering to support terrorism and other issues of that nature there would be a greater argument for biometrics across the mainstream of American businesses.

Question: What will be the major priorities during your tenure at the ETA in the coming two years?

©Performance Training Systems

MD: During my tenure at the ETA in the coming two years I will focus on high level exposure for the ETA to help improve the recognition and value of our members in the marketplace and position ETA as a key resource to policymakers. I will work to deploy our educational resources to the widest audience possible to help improve knowledge and best practices that critically impact merchant satisfaction. I will also continue ETA's initiatives to be an information warehouse for the current and future technology available in our industry. I will continue the close alliance with the card brands whose products and services are at the core of our existence.

Interview with Cynthia Dorrill Transaction World Magazine

Cynthia Dorrill is the Editor-in-Chief and Managing Publisher of *Transaction World* Magazine. An industry professional with 12 years experience in the acquiring side of the bankcard processing industry, she launched *Transaction World* in February 2001. She began her career at Nova Information Systems, in Atlanta, where she performed various product and marketing roles and later, at Lynk Systems, Inc. where she oversaw the marketing department. Ms. Dorrill resides in Atlanta, GA.

Question: Do you feel a salesperson entering in the industry now has the potential to earn a substantial income?

CD: Certainly. Perhaps not the same opportunity as existed 10 years ago where a relatively inexperienced salesperson could sell new hardware at huge margins to merchants who previously processed using a paper-based system, but opportunity still exists. A salesperson entering today's industry needs to use a different approach, a more consultative, service-oriented approach, to selling processing services.

Instead of going for the quick hardware sale and moving to the next merchant, a successful salesperson should provide a total solution to the merchant, that incorporates all his point-of-sale needs and that will tie that merchant to the salesperson for the long haul.

Today's new salesperson should ensure that he aligns himself with a reputable ISO or Acquirer, that he is knowledgeable about bankcard association rules, that he understands the merchant processing agreement and can explain it to the merchant, and that he brings the merchant affordable solutions that positively affect the merchant's business. So sure, the opportunity to make a successful living still exists, for the smart, informed salesperson.

Question: What advice would you give to a new salesperson entering the industry?

CD: First and foremost I would advise that he ensure that the company for which he is selling is reputable, that they provide significant training and ongoing support to both their sales teams and their merchants, and that he has the opportunity to earn residual income from merchants that stay with the company. I would also encourage new salespeople to seek out information about new products and solutions that can benefit merchants and that will provide them incentive to remain with the salesperson's company.

Questions: What skills are most critical to sales success in this industry?

CD: Generally the same skills that are critical to succeed in sales, also apply to our industry. Honesty, integrity, persistence, the desire to find appropriate solutions for your customers and the drive to succeed. Additionally, salespeople should have the wherewithal to educate themselves about industry rules and regulations, they should take it upon themselves to understand the anatomy of a transaction, they should understand funding and should realize that while critical to a merchant's success, most merchants don't want to really think about their credit card processing on a daily basis. They expect it to work when they need it to, like the phone and the electricity, and bogging them down with unnecessary equipment and functionality doesn't further the salesperson's goal of creating a beneficial long term relationship.

Question: How important is ongoing training in your opinion?

CD: It is critical. If the salesperson's company does not provide it, salespeople should seek it out on their own. With the rapidly changing regulations and with new products and services coming about, a successful salesperson is only as good as is his education about the industry and its products and services.

Question: What shape is the industry in right now?

CD: In my opinion the industry is near maturation. The number of players on the acquiring side is shrinking. However, I think this is a positive sign for the industry. It means that to be a significant player, you must come to the table with significant capabilities, one of which is a strategic plan to succeed, goals to grow your business and the desire to make that happen. The days when people haphazardly entered the industry to build a quick portfolio to sell and then retire on a beach somewhere are gone.

Today's industry players must recognize that, for the most part, merchants are more sophisticated about processing services. They have the equipment they need to operate their businesses and what they really need from their processor is reliable service at a fair price and access to upgrades and new products and services as would benefit them.

Anyone who has been in the industry for more than 5 years also knows that the sale of processing services has become a commodity – the true way to making a profit in today's industry is by providing the service the merchant needs and holding on to those merchants. With a normal attrition rate of around 33% a year, most processors spend over a third of their sales time just replacing the merchants that left. So the key to success is finding a way to keep those merchants and using sales as a tool to grow, not maintain the status quo.

Question: What do you think the future looks like in the industry?

CD: There will be fewer, but stronger, ISOs and Acquirers. We may see, in the next few years, more industry standards and a move towards salesperson certification, to provide both a benchmark for measuring success and to ensure compliance with industry appropriate behaviors. Certification of salespeople will also serve as a natural barrier to entry for new salespeople as they would have to undergo certain training and meet certain qualifications. This would professionalize the industry a great deal and be a benefit to the industry and merchants across the board. The question isn't really IS certification going to happen, it is more, who will oversee this process and enforce the rules and when it will all occur.

Interview with Mary Gerdts President of the ETA (2002-2003)

Mary Gerdts is currently the President of the ETA and is president and chief executive officer of POST Integration Inc. in Scottsdale, Arizona. POST Integrations provides electronic transaction services exclusively to the hospitality industry, integrating the financial, technical and operational transaction needs of hotels. Ms. Gerdts also serves on numerous charity and professional association boards

Question: Do you feel a salesperson entering in the industry now has the potential to earn a substantial income?

MG: Definitely. Income should be tied to an incentive program, not just new equipment sales and not necessarily tied to equipment period. A good sales rep can earn 60,000-80,000 per year based on there commission plan.

Question: What advice would you give to a new salesperson entering the industry?

MG: Become an expert in your field. Live, eat, breathe your industry.

Question: What tools do you think are most important for the field sales reps?

MG: Building relationships are the most important. If you take care of the relationship, that relationship will do the work for you. Relationships are critical regardless of what business you are in.

Question: What do you think the future looks like in the industry and salespeople?

MG: **The industry is ever changing. I've been in it 11 years now, and I believe the feet on the street will always be very, very important.**

Question: What products do you see coming out that will impact the industry the most, i.e. biometrics, smart cards?

MG: **The most practical product in the foreseeable Future is smart cards. Biometrics is a great product with regard to the current state of the country and terrorism. The issue is, will people embrace biometrics? Gift card and loyalty will continue to grow at a very rapid pace.**

Interview with Paul H. Green

Paul Green is chairman and editor in chief of The Green Sheet, Inc. a publishing company focused on providing education, inspiration and actionable advice for sales professionals in the payments processing industry. The Green Sheet, Inc. produces *The Green Sheet,* a bi-monthly magazine and *GSQ: The Payment Systems Authority*, as well as occasional books and seminars. As *The Green Sheet* approaches its 20th anniversary, it has become the most widely read publication in the payment processing industry. Published in print and online, this trade journal now reaches over 15,000 readers each issue and generates over 1,000,000 hits per month to the Web site. Paul's annual "U.S. Check Study," published six times, became the industry source for tracking trends in paper check usage. These reports culminated in the publication of his book, *Checks at the End of the 20th Century and Beyond*, the definitive study on the use of paper checks in the US. It continues to be frequently quoted in trade journals and economics textbooks. Paul also authored *Good Selling! A sales training and motivational manual for sales professionals.* The Green Sheet, Inc, published both books.

Paul was CEO of CrossCheck, Inc. from 1983 through 2001. He was president of Telecredit Check Services, Inc., prior to its acquisition by Equifax, and was responsible for that company's 300 million to 3 billion dollars a year growth. He holds a BA in Accounting and Computer Science, an MBA, and has been a Financial Executive Institute Member for over 20 years. In 2000 he was awarded the Republican Senatorial Medal of Freedom, "The highest honor the Republican members of the U.S. Senate can bestow." Paul is a noted lecturer, an acclaimed artist and art collector, an amateur classicist and biblical Historian, and world-class explorer. Paul has been happily married to his wife, Tischa, for over 30 years.

Question: Since you've been in the bankcard industry what major changes have you seen?

PG: I've been involved in the bankcard industry since the 1970s and founded the first Independent Sales Organization selling bankcard services in 1983. I've seen this industry move from knuckle-buster paper-driven processing to Web-based and wireless transactions. The evolution of bankcard acquiring from BankAmericard and MasterCharge to Visa and MasterCard, from paper to electronic, and from the high end merchant to "Everywhere you want to be" has been driven by the ISOs. All of the changes in this industry are a direct result of one decision, to move the merchant account sales from bankers to sales professionals.

Question: What do you think the future looks like in the industry?

PG: For the last 30 years, Visa and MasterCard (credit card) dollar volumes have shown positive year-over-year growth, and I expect this will continue. Even in the last two recessions, growth remained in the high single-digit to low double-digit range. The market for electronic payments is still wide open. In fact, I think that the dollar volume of card-based payments will grow at an average rate of 11% through 2010.

Question: As a distribution channel how important do you think the ISO and sales representative are to Visa/MasterCard?

PG: The sale of payment processing services and the POS equipment that makes the transactions possible is dependent on the ISO sales channel. Without the army of independent sales professionals in the US, much of the growth experienced by Visa and MasterCard would never have happened. Banks are not sales organizations. If the bean counters and risk-managers had maintained control over merchant account sales I believe BankAmericard would still be a regional conversation-piece for the wealthy.

Question: What are the major challenges facing the industry?

PG: There are several significant challenges facing the payments processing industry at this time, not the least of which is governmental investigation and possible regulatory statutes. The anti-trust action against Visa and MasterCard, FTC investigation of CMS, class-action litigation against the card associations, and statutory regulations affecting card receipts and tip reporting will all impact the economic strength of this industry. At this time it is not clear if real growth is still possible in the bankcard acquiring market or if it has become a net-sum game, with merchants and revenue simply moving from one player to another.

With an industry built on residual payments the ultimate challenge is to develop the service infrastructure that will enable the sales professional to do what he/she does best, sell.

Question: What tools do you think are most important for the field sales reps?

PG: The most important "tool" for any sales professional is a strong support team. Sales professionals are a special breed; their singular skill is to sell. A team that enables the salesperson to sell, and not be distracted with support and service will come out on top. "Sales" is the most difficult of professions. Few have the ego-strength to withstand the day-in and day-out grind of proposal and rejection that the sales professional must withstand. Not just "withstand," but actually thrive on the challenge of making the numbers. Nothing happens in this industry until a salesperson sells.

Question: What would be your advice to a new salesperson entering the business?

PG: **Winning in sales always results from the same simple process: hard work. Referrals or leads are nice, and interested prospects that call you out of the blue can make your day, but they are seldom a steady diet.**

Regardless of whether you are knocking on doors or smiling and dialing, nothing replaces the hard work of starting all over again tomorrow.

Question: What skills are most critical to sales success in this industry?

PG: **In all my years of sales and training sales professionals I've found that the most critical skill is to remember one thing. Ask for the sale.**

Interview With Gil Gillis

Gil is the founder of 1st National Bankcard Services Inc./1st National Processing Inc., a merchant bankcard marketing and point-of-sale equipment company that is one of the largest of its kind in the nation. Due to a recent merger/acquisition with another large transaction processor, this company has expanded to provide an extensive variety of corporate and merchant services to financial institutions, banks and thousands of merchants, who process millions of dollars monthly, nationwide.

During his 30 plus years, he has had many accomplishments in the sales and marketing industry; as an executive and an entrepreneur in a diverse range of trades including automotive aftermarket, wholesale and retail computer sales, computer software design and development.

Gil has a stalwart background in the military by serving his country in the United States Air Force with accommodations. Gil specialized in aircraft maintenance/electronic counter measures in Europe, Africa, the Middle East and Southeast Asia. Following his active duty in the Air Force, Gil served with the U. S. Department of Defense in a classified position.

Gil has been an active community member by dedicating his time and service to various organizations including the Simi Valley YMCA Board of Managers and the Masonic Lodge. Gil received academic honors from West Virginia University, Fairmont State Teachers' College in West Virginia, and West Texas State University.

Question: Do you feel a salesperson entering in the industry now has the potential to earn a substantial income?

GG: **Yes, but they need to partner with a**

processor who supports and understands sales on the street. There is always outstanding income potential in this industry. As the payment industry evolves so will the salesperson. Those salespeople that can hit the streets and get back to face to face selling will prosper the most.

Question: What advice would you give to a new salesperson entering the industry?

GG: Stick with it. Learn the industry and become a professional. Have yourself some time to learn the business and build your portfolio of accounts. I have known several guys that sold their portfolio for millions in 5 years or less.

Question: What skills are most critical to sales success in this industry?

GG: Prospecting, Persistence, Self Discipline. And learn good people skills. Its always been said that there are 3 key ingredients to success be in the right place, at the right time, with the right product certainly this industry provides all three. But there is a fourth with the right people. Hookup with a processor that provides all the tools you need to be successful. Training, Service and Support.

Question: How important is ongoing training in your opinion?

GG: Training is critical. Not only on the technical side of the business, but on the sales side as well. Sales reps need to understand what the merchants needs are and be able to present the solution to those needs in a professional and diligent manner. I believe a well trained rep is worth 5 untrained reps. With good training you can almost ensure their success.

Get trained by professionals like Bill and Marc. Always be willing to learn, after the initial training it doesn't stop there, you need to partner with a processor that provides on going training for you and your reps.

Question: What shape is the industry in right now?

GG: It's never been better. There is a lot of activity in the industry at this time and it is positive at all levels. In my opinion there is unlimited opportunity right now. We are in a recession proof industry; when things are good people use their cards to earn miles or rewards. When things are bad people use their cards to pay bills, we can't lose.

Question: What do you think the future looks like in the industry?

GG: I believe the future is unlimited. New products are being developed every day that will continue to entrench the sale rep in the merchant's place of business.

Question: What products do you see coming out that will impact the industry the most, i.e. biometrics, smart cards?

GG: The hottest trends are applications that target specific niche markets, such as medical insurance verification and patient bill payment. Smart cards and EBT are also starting to take off.

©Performance Training Systems

Interview with Lee Ladd

Mr. Ladd started in the finance business in 1961 at HFC. Moved to Fireside Thrift in 1963 and was Regional Vice President for Southern California when I left in 1979 to start Ladco Leasing. In 1984 was the first lesson to lease POS equipment. In 1986 pioneered ACH for POS lease payment. In 1990 we were the first to securitize a POS lease portfolio. I sold Ladco in 1997 to PMT Services, which was acquired by NOVA Information Services, which was acquired by US Bancorp, our current parent.

Question: Do you feel a salesperson entering in the industry now has the potential to earn a substantial income?

LL: Absolutely. There are millions of customers with outdated equipment and many have never seen their original agent since installation.

Question: What advice would you give to a new salesperson entering the industry?

LL: Be aligned with a solid ISO that has a great reputation for customer service and can produce MIDs quickly.

Question: What skills are most critical to sales success in this industry?

LL: The ability to sell and deliver service. Establish integrity and service and you will be assured of success.

Question: What shape is the industry in right now?

LL: Reasonably good. Need to continue the clean up to avoid government intervention.

Question: What do you think the future looks like in the industry?

LL: Bright. New products and new equipment equals great opportunity.

Question: What are the major challenges facing the leasing industry?

LL: Money, money, money. The easy money cycle is about to come to an end. A leasing company's delinquency and charge offs will dictate that company's future. Future money will be dependant on good historical statistics.

Question: What products do you see coming out that will impact the industry the most i.e. biometrics, smart cards?

LL: Virtually any product that the mass market will need or want that requires an equipment change or addition will impact both the ISO and leasing industry the most.

Any comments you'd like to add?

LL: It is time for the ISO community to realize that their future in sales is dependant on the lesson and its ability to fund future deals. If there is a major lease company failure it will reverberate throughout the industry and create havoc like no one has ever seen. I would visualize major funds drying up very quickly.

Wall Street is very aware of failure and future securitization (the source of most new money) would be in jeopardy.

Interview with Paul Martaus

Mr. Martaus is the president of Martaus & Associates, a company that specializes in electronic payment systems research consulting and professional education. The company's mission is to assist clients in determining appropriate courses of action to take in response to competitive threats and opportunities. It specializes in posing issues to the financial services industry through executive interviews and surveys and interpreting the results to the best advantage of its clients.

Since its inception in December of 1990, Martaus & Associates has performed a variety of engagements for clients evaluating the state of the credit card transaction acquisition industry, the ISO marketplace; and electronic commerce on the Internet; In addition, Martaus & Associates has provided extensive professional education for clients through numerous seminars and speaking engagements.

Mr. Martaus has over 20 years of direct banking operations and EFT experience and has directed numerous EFT and operations related projects. Mr. Martaus holds a BS in Finance and an MBA in Management.

Question: Looking at the way the majority of bankcard services are delivered today, through outside salespeople. Do think that model will continue to be strong?

PM: Yes. I would assume they would in that **acquirers have always kind of relied on some type of marketing arm to distribute their services.**

Comment: Makes sense. I agree totally, and especially with the new products in development, they're going to have to have someone out there with the merchant showing them how these products are going to impact their business.

PM: **Absolutely, absolutely**

Question: What do you think the new hotter products are going to be, gift, loyalty?

PM: ISOs are always looking for opportunities to increase their revenue flow. So, they're going to take these new innovations and say, "thank you very much. How much is it going to make me? If it doesn't make me bazillion dollars, I am not going to sell it!

Comment: I think you're right on target.

PM: **Now understand, I have some influence at many of these companies. I meet with their management teams all the time and I tell them the same thing every time I see them, "The independent sales organization I talked to yesterday said if you can get them POS terminal with a pin pad for 200 bucks, you don't have to do anything else, because you're rich. You're done, you're over."**

A theoretical discussion goes like this - Their eyes glaze over and they say, "We've got biometrics!!!" It's not germane. "We've got..." It doesn't matter! Is it cheap? Do the lights blink when you press the button, that's all the ISO salespeople seem to want. "No, No, No, really, we've got data", I don't care who you've got data from. I'm telling you what the salespeople told me. "I don't know who you've been talking to but that's not what we hear." Well, fine, go sell it to somebody else, then.

That's the issue. We have had a number of false starts. I have always thought that the PC would be the big seller. You know what, I was wrong. I really thought that after 9/11, the war on terrorism would shove identification right to the forefront. It did not. The same with check conversion. I really thought it was a go. It's not. Gift cards are a whole issue in and of itself.

Question: And, what do you mean by the gift card issue? The unredeemed gift amounts?

PM: Yes, there is a contingent liability on what's called a forward purchase amount. And, that's like buying an airline ticket.

Question: Oh, if they buy a gift card on a credit card?

PM: Yes, if they buy it with a credit card, then that contingent liability is owned by the person who sold it. Until the value is exhausted.

Comment: Right, if the merchant goes out of business, the customer can't redeem the gift card, they can dispute the charge and get their money back.

PM: Right. There you go.

Question: Right. That makes sense. How about loyalty, that seems like a great product.

PM: When I look at the gift card market or the loyalty market place, I have found that the American consumer, for some unknown reason, puts such a tremendous value on a free airline ticket that will "get you anywhere in the continental United States." Given that substantial of a reward, I can promise you that when you get on an airplane you make sure your miles have been logged.

Comment: Sure we do.

PM: And the reason that you do that is that you are also of the same belief of everybody else. That we have this incredibly valuable thing at our disposal and it's free. For the most part, however, most airline tickets are not extremely expensive. But we perceive that they are, thus we really keep track of those miles because the reward is special!

Now, many of the supermarket loyalty programs give you rewards for buying a loaf of bread. There's no glitz, there's no glamour, there's no "Oh my God, I get to go to any aisle in the supermarket and get groceries for free!" Who really cares? And, there's no pizzazz and there's no real belief that the value associated with that reward program is enough to sway my purchase decisions.

When we did consumer studies we learned is that consumers typically use three supermarkets. We have a primary that we shop in all the time. We also have a secondary and we'll shop there, but not quite as much as the primary. And, then we all have a third one that I call the specialty market where we buy something because it is the only place you could get the specific product.

In the supermarket industry scenario a loyalty kind of a program doesn't work because we don't seem to associate enough value there to shift our purchase behavior.

Comment: So, they're introducing these programs, but they don't have an increase in traffic.

PM: No, they don't.

Comment: So, the same sales dollars are being spent, no new dollars.

PM: There you go. Or, they're actually losing money because they are giving away a product at a discount, or they are giving you a gift with it, but it's not changing your behavior.

Comment: Right, you're not spending any more. So, they're losing more money.

PM: Correct. And, thus far it's been a dismal failure. You want to really get somebody upset or angry, go to a supermarket and talk to them about they're loyalty programs.

Comment: What about reward programs, maybe at a Blockbuster, get a 10th movie free, or an oil change…

PM: You're going to go there anyway; it's not going to change your behavior.

Question: Do you see any of that from the sales rep out in the field, even though it may not increase traffic, will it help that merchant advertise more? Possibly by having the card in their wallet or help build brand awareness?

PM: No, No, what's happening on the sales side is that every good ISO sales person is doing exactly what they should. And, what they are selling is smoke and mirrors, which is their stock in trade.

For the most part they don't really care if a service helps the merchant. You can't care about the merchant. You want to sell the terminal. You want to sell the increased revenue associated with selling whatever that program is. That's why pin based debit got a boost a while back, because you've got more money to put the pin pad in there, that's why check conversion sells, because you can place a check reader.

How many companies do you think that were sold check conversion still use it? I mean, 30-40-50% will be gone in the first year. But, in the mean time you got the revenue on placing the check reader.

And, that's what you want. You don't care about the rest of it. You want the revenue. You want the money that's associated with getting the deal closed. That's where your paycheck comes from and that's what makes your mortgage payment. Simple as that.

Comment: Well, that's definitely describes a lot of the guys in the field.

PM: That's the reason that we're getting some increased activity in some of these programs is because the independent sales organization sales guys are the ones out there selling it. And they do it because they get more revenue in their pocket. That's the reason, and it finally dawned on me after all these years of trying to figure it all out. Some new product or service might be really hot, and I see the flash. Wow! That one's going to be really hot. Then all of a sudden it's gone. And I sit back and ask, "Why did it fail?" Simply because it didn't boost the sales person's monthly check. And, it's gone now.

Appendix A – Income Goal Sheet

What is your yearly income goal? _____

What is your average commission per sale? _____

Divide your total income by your average Commission. This is your total sales goal for the year. _____

There are 49 working weeks per year. Divide the total number of sales by 49. This is your weekly sales goal. _____

What is your closing ratio per presentation? (If you don't know use 20% to be safe.) _____

Divide your weekly sales goal by your closing percentage (for this example divide sales 2.55 sales by .20= 12.75 presentations). This is the number of presentations that need to be made. _____

How many contacts do you need to make your weekly presentation goal?

What is your appointment ratio (how many Prospect contacts need to made to perform one sales presentation) (if you don't know use 10% as a worst case scenario) _____

Total weekly prospect contacts to meet your presentation goal (Divide weekly presentations by percentage) Example 12.75/.10 _____

Daily contacts required: (divide total by 5) _____

©Performance Training Systems

Appendix B - Daily Call Sheet

"I will do today what others won't, so tomorrow I can do what others can't."

Date: _____   **Start Time:** _____
                              End Time: _____

My Daily Total Calls Goal is: _____

1 2 3 4 5 6 7 8 9 10 11 12 13 14 15 16 17 18 19 20 21 22 23
24 25 26 27 28 29 30 31 32 33 34 35 36 37 38 39 40 41 42
43 44 45 46 47 48 49 50 51 52 53 54 55 56 57 58 59 60 61
62 63 64 65 66 67 68 69 70 71 72 73 74 75

New Prospect Calls:

1 2 3 4 5 6 7 8 9 10 11 12 13 14 15 16 17 18 19 20 21 22 23
24 25 26 27 28 29 30 31 32 33 34 35 36 37 38 39 40 41 42
43 44 45 46 47 48 49 50 51 52 53 54 55 56 57 58 59 60

Prospect Call Backs:

1 2 3 4 5 6 7 8 9 10 11 12 13 14 15 16 17 18 19 20

Joint Venture Calls:

1 2 3 4 5 6 7 8 9 10

Results

Sales:

1 2 3 4 5

©Performance Training Systems

Appointments:

1 2 3 4 5 6 7 8 9 10

Information Requests:

1 2 3 4 5 6 7 8 9 10 11 12 13 14 15 16 17 18 19 20

Follow up Calls Scheduled:

1 2 3 4 5 6 7 8 9 10 11 12 13 14 15 16 17 18 19 20

©Performance Training Systems

Appendix C – Developing a Telemarketing Script

Use this format to help develop the right telemarketing script. This is just a general template. Try new scripts until you find the one that works.

Attention!

1. Develop an Initial Benefit Statement.

Qualify

2. May I ask you a few quick questions?

Are you aware that rates have been increased again?
Are you aware that smart cards are coming out?
Did you know that you don't have to pay the normal percentage on a check card transaction?
Have thought about offering gift cards to your customers?
Were you aware that it cost 7 times more to find a new customer than to sell to an existing customer?
Are you having a problem with returned checks?
If I had a way to …… would you ……?

Social Proof

3. We have been able to ……(demonstrate a benefit) for (other clients, hundreds) of people, etc.

Take Away (optional)

4. I'm not sure we can help you……or….. We can't help everyone we meet.

Offer

5. I am willing to invest 15 minutes to determine if you can benefit, qualify or are a candidate….or…..to brainstorm, discuss ideas, etc.

Concession

6. I'm not going to ask you to buy….or….I'm not going to sell you anything.

Promise

7. If I cannot save you money, make you money, improve, help your situation in some way…I will not take anymore of your valuable time and….I will not ask for your business! Is that fair?

Commitment

8. Set Appointment

Reinforce, Reassure

9. You're really going to like/enjoy/appreciate what I've got to show you/share with you….or the time we spend. Thank You

EXAMPLE:

Hi is the owner in? Hi this is _____with_____ the reason for my call is to make you aware of a new program that we have developed to increase customer loyalty and profits, do you mind if I ask you a couple quick questions to see if I can help you? Thanks.

Are you aware that it costs roughly 7 times more to acquire a new customer than it does to sell to an existing customer?

We have developed several innovative products that have been able to help businesses in your area retain existing customers and not lose them to competitors.

I'm not sure if we can help you, we can't help everyone but I would be willing to drop by for 15 minutes to discuss our customer retention program with you. If I can't help you increase your bottom line I won't take up any of your valuable time and I certainly won't ask for your business is that fair?

Great, I'm available Tuesday at 3:00 or Wednesday at 10:00am which time works best for you.

Great Wednesday at 10:00 it is, and I'm sure you find what I have to share will benefit your business.

©Performance Training Systems

Appendix D – Sample Client Questionnaire

1. How long have you been in business? Or when are you planning on opening?

2. How do you advertise or how are you planning to advertise?

3. Have you spoken to any other merchant service providers?

4. What did you like most about their program?

5. What didn't you like most about their program?

6. Have you every used a credit card terminal?

7. What type of monthly volume do feel you will process?

8. What is your average sale amount?

9. What is your target date to implement a system?

10. What is most important to you when considering the purchase of a payment system?

11. How do you know when you have _____?

12. If I could show you a program that gives you_____, and makes sense for you, not me, would you consider doing business today?

12. If no, what else is most important to you when making a purchasing decision?

Customize your questions based on the products you want to offer.

Appendix E - Pain and Pleasure Exercise

List 3 reasons why your customer will continue to experience pain **today** if they don't use your products and services.

1. _____
2. _____
3. _____

List 3 reasons why your customer will experience pleasure or gain **today** from doing business with you today.

1. _____
2. _____
3. _____

List 3 **futures** your customer could experience if they don't use your products and services.

1. _____
2. _____
3. _____

List 3 **futures** bright futures your customer will experience by using your products and services.

1. _____
2. _____
3. _____

©Performance Training Systems

Appendix F – Preventing Objections Worksheet

Objection:
_____

Answer:
_____

_____

_____

Prove It:
_____

Objection:
_____

Answer:
_____

_____

_____

Prove It:
_____

Objection:
_____

Answer:
_____

_____

_____

Prove It:
_____

Objection:
_____

Answer:
_____

_____

_____

Prove It:
_____

Repeat as many exercises as needed.

Appendix G – Advertising 101

> *"Genius is one percent inspiration and ninety-nine percent perspiration."*
> *- Thomas Alva Edison*

For our purposes advertising will include classified ads, print media (i.e. yellow pages, magazines) and direct mail pieces.

In order to get your prospects Attention, Interest and Motivate them to action a Unique Selling Proposition (USP) must be developed. Rosser Reeves introduced this concept in his book "Reality in Advertising".

The three elements that every USP must contain are:

- Each advertisement must make a proposition to the consumer. Each advertisement must say to the reader: 'Buy this product, and you will get this specific benefit."

- The proposition must be one that the competition either cannot, or does not, offer. It must be unique -- either a uniqueness of brand or a claim not otherwise made in that particular field."

- The proposition must be so strong that it can move people to action, i.e., pull over new customers to your product."

Why do you need a USP? In almost every field, from accounting to online marketing, competitors are plentiful.

If your product is not differentiated from your competition's in a way that is unique, better, and useful to the buyer, why should they call you instead of the competition?

The USP is the compelling reason why people should prefer you to other competitors in the merchant services industry.

How to write a good advertisement

This is a reprint from one of the top copyrighters in the business Robert Bly. He is a freelance copywriter specializing in business-to-business and direct response advertising. He writes ads, brochures, direct mail packages, and sales letter for more than 75 clients nationwide including Prentice-Hall, Grumman Corporation, Sony, Online Software, Digital Linguistix, and Philadelphia National Bank. He is also the author of 17 books including The Copywriter's Handbook (Dodd, Mead). Bly can be reached at 174 Holland Ave., New Milford, NJ 07646 - 201/599-2277.

To define what constitutes good print advertising, we begin with what a good print ad is not:

- **It is not creative for the sake of being creative.**
- **It is not designed to please copywriters, art directors, agency presidents or even clients.**
- **Its main purpose is not to entertain, win awards or shout at the readers, "I am an *ad*. Don't you admire my fine writing, bold graphics and clever concept?"**

In other words, ignore most of what you would learn as a student in any basic advertising class or as a trainee in one of the big Madison Avenue consumer ad agencies.

Okay. So that's what an ad shouldn't be. As for what an ad *should* be, here are some characteristics shared by successful direct response print ads:

They stress a benefit. The main selling proposition is not cleverly hidden but is made immediately clear. Example: "How to Win Friends and Influence People."

They arouse curiosity and invite readership. The key here is not to be outrageous but to address the strongest interests and concerns of your target audience. Example: "Do you Make These Mistakes in English?" appeals to the reader's desire to avoid embarrassment and write and speak properly.

They provide information. The headline "How to Stop Emission Problems - at Half the Cost of Conventional Air Pollution Control Devices" lures the reader because it promises useful information. Prospects today seek specific, usable information on highly specialized topics. Ads that provide information the reader wants get higher readership and better response.

They talk to the reader. Why are so many successful control ads written by direct response entrepreneurs rather the top freelance copywriters and direct response agencies?

My theory is that when people see a non-direct response ad, they know it's just a reminder-type ad and figure they don't have to read it.

Because, although these entrepreneurs may not be professional writers, they know their product, their audience and what holds their audiences' interest. And that is far more important than copywriting technique or style.

They are knowledgeable. Successful ad copy reflects a high level of knowledge and understanding of the product and the problem it solves. An effective technique is to tell the reader something he already knows, proving that you, the advertiser, are well versed in his industry, application or requirement.

An opposite style, ineffectively used by many "professional" agency copywriters, is to reduce everything to the simplest common denominator and assume the reader is completely ignorant. But this can insult the reader's intelligence and destroy your credibility with him.

They have a strong free offer. Good ads contain a stronger offer. They tell the reader the next step in the buying process and encourage him to take it **NOW.**

All ads should have an offer, because the offer generates immediate response and business from prospects that are ready to buy now or at least thinking about buying. Without an offer, these "urgent" prospects are not encouraged to reach out to you, and you lose many potential customers.

In addition, strong offers increase readership because people like ads that offer them something - especially if it is free and has high perceived value.

Writers of image advertising may object, "But doesn't making an offer cheapen the ad, destroy our image? After all, we want awareness, not response." But how does offering a free booklet weaken the rest of the ad? It doesn't, of course. The entire notion that you cannot simultaneously elicit a response and communicate a message is absurd and without foundation.

They are designed to emphasize the offer.

Graphic techniques such as "kickers" or eyebrows (copy lines above the headline), bold headlines, liberal use of subheads, bulleted or numbered copy points, coupons, sketches of telephone, toll-free numbers set in large type, pictures of response booklets and brochures, dashed borders, asterisks, and marginal notes make your ads more eye-catching and response-oriented, increasing readership.

They are clearly illustrated. Good advertising does not use abstract art or concepts that force the reader to puzzle out what is being sold. Ideally, you should be able to understand *exactly* what the advertiser's proposition is within five seconds of looking at the ad. As John Caples observed a long time ago, the best visual for an ad for a record club is probably a picture of records.

At about this point, someone from DDB will stand up and object: "Wait a minute. You said these are the characteristics of a successful *direct response* ad. But isn't general advertising different?"

Maybe. But one of the ways to make your general advertising more effective is to **write and design it as a direct response ad.** Applying all the stock-in-trade techniques of the direct marketer (coupons, toll-free numbers, free booklets, reason-why copy, benefit-headlines, informative subheads) virtually guarantees that your advertisement will be better read - and get more response - than the average "image" ad.

7 Ways to Create Business Publication Advertising that Gets Results

How do you create an industrial or trade ad that gets attention, wins high readership scores, and generates a steady flow of valuable inquiries that convert easily to sales?

Here are some ideas, based on study (conducted to gather material for my book, *Ads That Sell*) of some advertisements that have proven successful in the marketplace:

Put a benefit in the headline.

The most successful ad I ever wrote (which was the number one inquiry producer in four consecutive insertions) had the headlines:

> HOW TO SOLVE YOUR EMISSIONS PROBLEMS...
> ... at *half the energy cost* on conventional venturi scrubbers.

The headline combines a powerful benefit ("half the energy cost") with the promise of useful information ("how to") addressed directly at the reader's specific problem ("solve *your* emissions problems").

Ask a provocative question.

My friend Bob Pallace wrote an ad that generated an immediate $1 million increase in billings for his ad agency in Silver Spring, Maryland. The headline was:

> ARE YOU TIRED OF WORKING FOR
> YOUR AD AGENCY?

The ad ran only one time in each of three magazines (*High-Tech Marketing, Business Marketing, Inc.*) and immediately brought in five new clients.

Be direct.

An ad agency asked me to write an ad to generate sales leads for a client that repairs and restores old surgical tables.

When they sent me their literature, I used the headline on their brochure as the headline for the ad.
It read:

> SURGICAL TABLES REBUILT
> Free Loaners Available

The ad was successful, and demonstrates that when you are the only one advertising a particular product or service, or when the nature of your offer is hard to grasp, direct headlines can be extremely effective. Another direct headline I like appeared in an ad running in *Network World:*

> LINK 8 PCS TO YOUR MAINFRAME
> ONLY $2,395

Donald Reddy, president of the firm, said the ad was extremely effective in generating a small but steady flow of highly qualified sales leads.

Give the reader useful information.

One way to increase readership is to promise the reader useful information in your headline, then deliver it in your ad copy.

For an ad offering business people a book on how to collect overdue bills, Milt Pierce wrote this headline:

> 7 WAYS TO COLLECT YOUR
> UNPAID BILLS.
> New from Dow Jones-Irwin...
> A Successful and Proven Way
> to Get Your Bills Paid Faster.

The information-type ad is highly effective in business-to-business advertising. Why? Because the reason business

©Performance Training Systems

people read trade journals is for information, not entertainment.

Offer a free booklet, brochure, or information kit.

Offering something tangible - a brochure, booklet, information kit, videotape, audiocassette, research report, checklist, or other material the reader can send for - has never failed to increase response for me in nearly a decade of ad writing.

At the end of your ad, put in a subhead offering the material (for example: "Get the facts - FREE!"). Then describe your brochure or booklet, show a picture of it, and explain what the reader must do to get it.

If you can add something to a sales brochure to make it of lasting value, so much the better. More people will request your piece and more people will keep it.

Use a coupon.

Coupons visually identify your ad as "direct response," causing more people to stop and read it (because they know that coupon ads usually offer free things of value). If the ad is one-third page or less, put a dashed border around the entire ad to create the feel and appearance of a coupon. Copy then instructs the reader. "For more information, clip this ad and mail with your business card to, {company name, address}."

Use a headline with multiple parts

A headline does not have to contain just one sentence or phrase set in one uniform type size. Often, you can create a more eye catching and effective headline using what I essentially call a three-part headline.

The first part, or kicker, is an "eyebrow or short line that goes in the upper left corner of the ad, either straight or at a slant. One good use of the kicker is to select a specific type of reader for the ad (e.g., "Attention COBOL Programmers"). Another effective technique is to let the reader know you are offering something free ("Special Free Offer - See Coupon Below").

Next, set in larger type, comes your mail headline, which states your central benefit that makes a powerful promise. Then, in the subhead, you expand on the benefit or reveal the specific nature of the promise. Examples:

> $500 A DAY WRITER'S UTOPIA
> Here's the breakthrough offer that opens up a whole new world for writers or those who hope to become writers:
>
> FOR HIGH SPEED HIGH PERFORMANCE DATA INTEGRATION, LOOK INTO MAGI MIRROR. Now you can move data instantly from one program to another right from your PC screen.

If your headline is designed to arouse curiosity or grab attention and does so at the expense of clarity, then be sure to make the nature of your proposition immediately clear in a subhead or within the first sentence. Otherwise you will lose the interest of the reader whose attention you worked so hard to gain.

Appendix H – Industry Internet Resources

Associations & Organizations

American Bankers Assoc.	www.aba.com/default.htm
Check Fraud Org.	www.ckfraud.org
Electronic Check Council	http://ecc.nacha.org
Electronic Transaction Association (ETA)	www.electran.org
Identity Theft	www.identitytheft.org
NACHA	www.nacha.org
Smart Card Alliance	www.smartcardalliance.org

Credit Card Company Sites

American Express	www.americanexpress.com
Diners Club	www.dinersclubnewsroom.com
Discover Card	www.discoverbiz.com
JCBN Card	www.jcbusa.com
MasterCard international	www.MasterCard.com
Visa	www.visa.com

Credit Card & ECommerce News

Bank Technology News
   www.banktechnews.com/btn/m_btn2.shtml

Card Technology News   www.cardtechnology.com

Card Forum   www.cardforum.com

Card Web   www.cardweb.com
Dove Consulting   www.consultdove.com

Epay News   www.epaynews.com

Internet.com   www.internet.com

The Greensheet   www.greensheet.com

UT of Austin   http://cism.bus.utexas.edu

ECommerce Research

Retail News   www.retailindustry.about.com

Equipment Distributors

DataCap   www.datacapsystems.com
Hypercom   www.hypercom.com
Ingenico   www.ingenico.com
Lipman (Nurit)   www.lipmanusa.com
Magtek   www.magtek.com
Mist Wireless   www.mistwireless.com
Schlumberger   www.smartcards.net
Thales   www.thales-e-trans.com
Verifone   www.verifone.com

Fraud Research

American Express

http://home5.americanexpress.com/merchant/resources/fraudprevention/datafraud_index.asp?merch_home=fraud_prev

MasterCard

www.MasterCardintl.com/merchant
www.MasterCardmerchant.com/preventing_fraud/index.html

Visa

www.usa.visa.com/business/merchants/fraud_basics_index.html

Merchant Fraud Squad	www.merchantfraudsquad.com
Consumer Id theft	www.consumer.gov/idtheft
Check Fraud	www.diogenesllc.com/checkfraud.pdf

Fed Site Check Fraud
   www.clev.frb.org/ccca/fo1q96/fraud.htm

Government Sites

Fed Chicago
   www.chicagofed.org/paymentsystems/index.cfm

Federal Trade Comm.	www.ftc.gov
Federal Reserve Site	www.frbservices.org

Online Sticker and POS Signage

American Express

http://home5.americanexpress.com/merchant/market/freedecals/freedecals_index.asp?merch_home=decalslogos

Discover
www.discoverbiz.com

Diners

www.dinersclubnorthamerica.com/US/en/diners_club.jhtml?pageId=us_04_01_99_01&topicCode=ms

MasterCard
www.MasterCardintl.com/brand/decals.html

Visa
www.visafulfillment.com/visamerchant

Appendix I - Tools You Can Use

Checkout these tools for success:

www.bni.com - Business lead exchange group.

www.briantracy.com - lot's of motivational and sales tips newsletters.

www.delorme.com - leads on CD for the whole country. Retail price $99.95. You can only export 1,000 names at a time.

www.efax.com - Free fax number that sends the fax to your email. For $9.95 you can upgrade to a local fax number and fax from you desktop.

Contact Management software here are two of the best: Goldmine at www.frontrange.com and ACT at www.act.com.

Demographics data – www.census.gov and www.demographics.com both are great sites to see where markets are growing.

www.getresponse.com/45256 - Free auto responder for follow up with your customers and email courses. Option to upgrade to more robust version.

Goal Setting Software – Goal Pro - www.goalpro.com/index.cfm?ID=50954 this is one of the best goal setting packages we've seen.

www.goleads.com - for $9.95 per month unlimited business leads (existing businesses only) in your area. Search by Zip, Phone or SIC code.

www.franklincovey.com - great time management tools.

www.freedomvoice.com/20067 - One phone number for your office, fax with follow me roaming.

www.mapquest.com - Free map and driving directions to your appointments.

www.nightingale.com - Excellent sales and personal growth programs.

www.optimist.org - join an optimist club.

www.winfaxpro.com - top notch faxing program (faxing from your PC). Great cover sheets.

www.yahoo.com - Free email to reach your customers.

Industry Glossary

ABA Routing Number

The American Banking Association (ABA) routing number is a unique, bank-identifying number that directs electronic ACH deposits to the proper bank. This number precedes the account number printed at the bottom of a check and is usually printed with magnetic ink.

ACH

Automated Clearing House is an electronic payment Network that exchanges funds via Electronic Funds Transfer (EFT) throughout the U.S. Over 98% of the nation's banks including the Federal Reserve belong to the ACH. ACH is the paperless funds transfer system maintained by the Federal Reserve or other entities that have networks to exchange electronic funds transfer items.

ACH Associations

Provide rules and guideline for the efficient operation of the ACH Network. There are 36 regional ACH associations whose memberships include financial institutions and affiliates. NACHA, the National Automated Clearing House Association forms the governing foundation for the regional associations.

ACH Network

The ACH network was established in the 1970s to facilitate direct deposit of military payroll and other federal payments. The network is made up of four central clearing facilities. In addition to three private sector facilities, the Federal Reserve became a central clearing house under the Monetary Control

Act of 1980. The Monetary Control Act required the Federal Reserve to make its center clearing services available to all financial institutions and required it to price those services. The Federal Reserve now processes 1/3 of all paper checks, and around 80% of all ACH transactions.

Acquirer

Any bank, financial institution, and public or private company that maintains a seller's credit card processing relationship and receives all transactions from the seller to be distributed to the credit card issuing banks.

Acquirer Payment Gateway

System operated by an acquirer for the purpose of providing electronic commerce services to merchants who interface with the acquirer for authorizing and capturing transactions.

Address Verification (AVS)

A service provided in which the seller verifies the cardholder's address with the Issuing Bank. Address Verification does not guarantee that a transaction is valid. The codes are as follows:

Y	Exact Match	Street and zip code match
A	Partial Match	Street matches, zip does not
Z	Partial Match	Zip code match, address does not match
N	No Match	Nothing matches
U	Unavailable	Information is unavailable
R	Retry	Issuer auth system is unavailable, retry later.

Agent Bank

A bank that participates in another bank's card issuing program. This bank turns over the merchant applications to the processing bank and acts as a depository for merchants.

American Express

An organization that issues cards and acquires transactions, unlike Visa and MasterCard, which are bank associations.

Approval Code

A code issued by the card-issuing bank allowing a sale to be charged against the cardholder's account. Approvals are requested via an authorization.

Associations

Visa and Mastercard are members of the associations. They establish and administer rule and regulations for the credit card industry.

Authorization

The request to charge a cardholder for goods or services. Authorization must be settled in order to post the authorization to the cardholder's account. If not processed within a certain time frame authorizations will be cancelled. The time period is usually from 3-7 days.

Auth Only (Pre Auth)

A transaction in which the merchant does not intend to charge the cardholder until a later date. For instance if the merchant is running a bar tab he may want to see if a

$100.00 charge is good, so he would obtain a pre auth to verify an open to buy.

Average Ticket

The average amount of each sale made by a merchant.

B2B

Business-to-business commerce.

Basis Point

One one-hundredth of a percent (.0001). Discount rates are expressed as basis points.

Batch

A collection of credit card transactions saved for submitting at one time, usually each day. Merchants who do not have real-time verification systems must submit their transactions manually through a POS terminal. Batch fees are charged to encourage a merchant to submit his or her transactions at one time, rather than throughout the day.

Batch ID

Once a batch is settled, it receives a batch ID. Every transaction in the batch shares this ID. If a transaction does not have a batch ID associated with it, the transaction has not been settled.

Batch Processing

A type of data processing where related transactions are transmitted as a group for processing.

Batch Settlement

An electronic bookkeeping procedure that causes all funds from captured transactions to be routed to the merchant's acquiring bank for deposit. Batches are settled from the terminal either manually or on auto-close.

BIN (Bank Identification Number)

The 6-digit range of numbers assigned by the Federal Bureau of Standards and used by card companies to identify their financial transactions. The Discover® range begins with '6' (6xxxxx), the MasterCard® range begins with '5' (5xxxxx), and the Visa® range begins with '4' (4xxxxx).

Bundled Rate

A discount rate that includes communications costs as well as transaction fees. Also referred to as a flat rate.

CDPD (Cellular Digital Package Data)

Wireless network owned by At&t and Verizon.

Card Validation Code (CVC)

This is a tool is used by Mastercard to prevent fraud. It requires that a number usually located on the back of the card above the magstripe be entered in to verify the card is present and authentic.

Card Verification Value (CVV or CVV2)

Card Verification Value Service is used by Visa and is a three digit security number indent printed on the back of Visa cards to help validate two things: that the customer has a genuine visa card in their possession and that the card account is legitimate.

CVV – Procedure

Each transaction needs to include one of the following from the merchant:

1. CVV is intentionally not provided.
2. CVV is present.
3. CVV is present but illegible.
4. Cardholder states that no CVV value is on the card.

The CVV Response from the bank will be:

1. CVV match.
2. CVV no match.
3. Not Processed.
4. Merchant has indicated the CVV is not on the card.
5. Card Issuer is not certified and/or on the system.

Capture

The act of creating an electronic transaction. Captured transactions are ready for settlement.

Card Issuing Bank

The financial institution that issues a credit card to a consumer. They are responsible for billing and collections to the cardholder.

Card-not-present

A merchant environment where the cardholder (and the card) is not physically present at the time of purchase. Typical card-not-present transactions take place in businesses focused on mail order/telephone order, business-to-business, and Internet-based transactions.

Card-present

A situation where the cardholder (and the card) is physically present at the time of purchase.

Chargeback

The act of reversing a sale made by the merchant. This can happen for many reasons including procedural and fraud. The process usually begins with a dispute from the cardholder.

Chargeback Period

The number of days a merchant can be chargeback.

Check Conversion or Truncation

The process of scanning and electronically transmitting the MICR line of a check from the POS terminal to the paying bank for settlement. The check is processed similar to a credit card transaction and is ACH debited from the customer's checking account.

Check Guarantee

Service that guarantees the amount of a check written to the merchant. Check guarantee companies will set the merchant's check limit and provide approval codes. If the check is returned the check guarantee company will refund back to the merchant the amount of the bad check. This service can usually be programmed on the merchant credit card terminal.

Check Reader

A hardware device that the check is passed thru in order to read the routing and account number and transmitted to the terminal for processing. Check readers are used to decreased user error and speed up processing time.

Check Verification

A service that verifies that the check writer has no outstanding bad checks in their database. If the check is returned the merchant is responsible for collecting the insufficient check.

Clearing

The exchange of data between the Acquirer and Issuer. This data is then posted to the cardholder account and reconciliation takes place.

Close Batch

The process by which transactions from the merchant are sent to the processor for payment.

Code "10" Authorization:

This is a voice authorization code for Visa that the merchant may initiate when they suspect a card is stolen or fake, or when a customer is acting suspiciously.

Credit or Return

A return of funds posted by the merchant back to the cardholder. These funds will be take from the merchant's bank account and posted by to the cardholder's account.

Credit Grade

The measure of a customer or businesses credit worthiness. This will determine your lease funding factor. Normal grades are usually A,B,C,D and E. Check with your leasing company for grading criteria and grades.

DUKPT

Derived Unique Key Per Transaction. Pin pad key management method.

Debit (On-line)

An ATM card used to purchase goods, services or obtain cash. The amount is debited from the cardholder's deposit account at their bank. Requires a PIN (personal identification number) for use.

Debit (Off-line)

An ATM card used to purchase goods or services. The amount is debited from the cardholder's deposit account at their bank. DOES NOT require a PIN (personal identification number) for use. These are called a check cards.

Decline

A response from the issuing bank that they will not approve the transaction.

Digital Certificate

A data file that contains information specific and unique to the certificate's owner. The certificates are issued by third-party certification authorities. When you receive the digital certificate from a customer, you contact the certification authority to unscramble the file, and verify the identity of the sender.

Discount rate

This is the percentage of the total transaction amount that is charged to the merchant to accept the credit card sale. Discount rates vary depending on the type of business and how the card is accepted. Discount rate includes dues and assessments and interchange.

Draft/Sales Draft:

A record (usually paper) used to document that goods or services were purchased.

Electronic Benefits Transfer (EBT)

The electronic transfer of insurance, food program or state benefits.

Electronic Check Conversion (ECC)

Electronic Check Council (Also ECC)

A program of NACHA, the ECC designs, proposes and monitors pilot programs for electronic payment services that enable the conversion of paper checks to electronic entries conveniently, reliably, securely and at an affordable cost. ECC also provides information on check conversion, as well as legal and regulatory matters.

Electronic Check Imaging

The process where the retailer can scan, capture and store an exact image of the consumer's check, enabling it to be downloaded should the need arise due to a returned ACH.

Electronic Draft Capture (EDC)

Entering and processing the sales drafts by electronic means. In online payment schemes, capture is used to denote the electronic deposit of the sales draft with the acquiring bank. System in which the transaction data is captured at the merchant location for processing and storage. The storage of information in a terminal's memory to be forwarded to a host computer at a later time. Process of electronically authorizing, capturing and settling a credit card transaction.

Electronic Funds Transfer (EFT)

Electronic Funds Transfer is the transfer of funds from one bank account to another bank account utilizing the ACH Network.

Europay, Mastercard, Visa (EMV)

Standard developed to allow cross payments and interoperability between Europe and Mastercard and Visa.

Fair Market Value (FMV)

The worth of a product at any given time in the marketplace. Refers to the fair market value at the end of a lease term. Fair market value is usually determined by a set formula provided by the lease company. This is the amount the merchant will pay to own the equipment at the end of the lease term.

Force

A transaction from which the merchant received a voice authorization. This allows the merchant to post the sale and settle the transaction. Also known as a post authorization.

Gateway or Payment Gateway

A payment gateway is a combination of hardware and software that provides merchants with the ability to perform real-time credit card authorizations from a website over the Internet. It's the link between a merchant website and the processor.

Gift Card

A prepaid card that is loaded with a specific amount that the cardholder can spend at the sponsoring retailer.

Global System for Mobile Communication (GSM)

Digital or PCS standard used primarily in Europe and Asia.

High Risk

A merchant that is considered a high risk based upon the credit, product, method, ticket size or volume. Examples of high-risk merchants are telemarketing, adult and travel related industries.

Host Capture

Type of transaction capture where the transaction information is stored at the processor's host computer system. Settle occurs at the processor level.

Host Computer

The computer system located at the processor that is dialed for authorization and settlement.

Independent Sales Organization (ISO)

ISOs act as a third party between the merchant and the acquiring bank. ISOs must register with Visa/MasterCard.

Industry Service Provider (ISP)

Independent companies who offer credit card processing services to merchant banks (i.e., FDR, NDC, VISANET).

Imprint

A physical impression of the customer's credit card. This proves that the card was present when the sale was made. The imprint is made with a device called an imprinter.

Note: An imprint can be created electronically by using a magnetic-stripe-reading terminal at the point-of-sale.

Interchange

The exchange of debit and credit transaction data between merchant banks and cardholder banks based on an agreement (governed by BASE II [VISA] or INET [MasterCard]) between the participants. The fees charged by the Issuer to the Acquirer.

Issuer

A bank that issues credit cards to consumers.

Lease

A contract between a lessor (lease company) and lessee (merchant) allowing the lessee to use the equipment for a specified time period.

Lease Factor

A number that is used to compute the gross funding amount of a lease. Factors are based upon lease term and credit rating of the merchant.

Lessee

The renter of the property described in the lease (the merchant).

Lessor

The owner or controller of the equipment being leased (lease company).

Loss Destruction Waiver (L&D Waiver)

A stipulation in the lease indicating that the lease company will cover the equipment if it is lost or damaged. There is an additional monthly fee associated with the L&D waiver.

Loyalty Card

A retailer or brand specific card that has cardholder benefits used to build brand or store loyalty. Cardholders are usually given an award or discount based upon number of visits or dollars spent.

Magnetic Ink Character Recognition (MICR)

The row of numbers printed at the bottom of a check that identifies the financial institution, account number, and check number. A check's MICR line can be scanned into a MICR reader, which translates it into a format that can be sent electronically.

Magnetic Stripe

A stripe on the back of a credit card that contains magnetically encoded cardholder information. The name of the cardholder is stored on Track I. The account number and expiration data are stored on Track II.

Manual Entry

Cardholder credit card information that is entered manually rather than swiped through the credit card terminal.

Mail Order/ Telephone Order (MOTO)

A type of payment card transaction where the order and payment information is transmitted to the merchant either by mail or by telephone. This a card not-present transaction.

Member Alert to Control High-Risk (MATCH)

System used to track merchants in order to manage risk.

Member Bank

A financial institution that is a member of Visa and/or MasterCard International. They are licensed to issue cards and/or accept merchant drafts.

Merchant

A business that accepts credit cards for goods or services.

Merchant Agreement

The written contractual agreement between a merchant and processor/acquirer containing their respective rights, duties, and warranties with respect to the acceptance of credit cards.

Merchant Identification Number (MID)

A number that numerically identifies each merchant to the merchant processor for accounting and billing purposes.

Merchant Statement

A summary produced and mailed at specified intervals, usually monthly, which details debits and credits to the merchant depository account.

MERIT

Qualification levels for Mastercard transactions. Standard, Merit I, Merit III, Merit III – being the highest rate.

National Automated Clearing House Association (NACHA)

The National Automated Clearing House Association is the chief rule making and interpretation body of the ACH. NACHA is the cooperative governing body for 36 regional ACH associations. www.nacha.org

Non-Qualified

A broad term that describes a transaction that did not interchange at the best rate because it was entered manually, not settled in a timely manner, or the data set required for the best interchange was not provided.

Offline

Mode when the merchant is not connected to the processor.

Open to Buy

The amount the cardholder has available on their credit card.

Originator

A company or other business entity that creates entries for introduction into the ACH network. For example, a billing company produces debit entries from customers' financial institution accounts who have authorized direct payment for products and services.

Personal Communication System (PCS)

Digital wireless communication system that operates on a different frequency range. Used by sprint.

Personal Digital Assistant (PDA)

Hand held digital assistant.

Personal Identification Number (PIN)

Personal Identification Number used by a cardholder to authenticate card ownership for ATM or debit card transactions. The cardholder enters his/her PIN into a PIN pad. The PIN is required to complete an ATM/debit card transaction.

Pin Entry Devices (PED)

A device used to enter a customer pin number.

Point of Sale (POS)

The time and place a sale takes place. Also refers to the devices used to transmit the credit card transaction.

Pre-Auth

The process of authorizing a card and reserving funds against the open to buy before a service is rendered by the merchant.

Pre-Notification

Prior to the initiation of the first ACH entry to an ACH receiver or the ACH receiver's account with an RDFI, an ACH originator may, at its option, deliver or send a pre-notification through an ODFI to its ACH operator for transmittal to the appropriate RDFI. The pre-notification provides notice to the RDFI that the originator intends to initiate one or more entries to that receiver's account in accordance to the receiver's authorization.

Private Label Card

A card that can be used only in a specific merchant's store.

Processor

A large data center that processes credit card transactions and settles funds to merchants. A processor connects to the merchant on behalf of an acquirer via a gateway or POS system to process payments electronically. Processors edit and format messages and switch to bankcard networks. They provide files for clearing and settlement and other value-added services.

Quick Service Restaurant (QSR)

Qualification

A level at which a transaction interchanges. Level of qualification is dependent on how the credit card number is entered, how quickly a transaction is settled, the type of industry, specific information, etc.

Radio Frequency Identification (RFID)

Customer card data is transferred via a chip/antenna on the credit card to the payment terminal, i.e. ExxonMobil SpeedPass, paypass.

Receipt

A hard copy of the description of the transaction that took place.

Receiver

A consumer, customer, employee, or business that has authorized ACH payments by Direct Deposit or Direct Payment to be applied against a depository account.

Receiving Depository Financial Institution (RDFI)

A financial institution that provides depository account services to consumers, employees, and businesses and accepts electronic debits and credits to and from those accounts.

Recurring Payment (RP)

A transaction authorized by the cardholder to occur for a specific amount at a specific time. For example, a monthly health club membership.

Return

A sale that is being credited back to the cardholder.

Retrieval Request

A request from a cardholder's bank for information about a charge, which is being disputed. Retrieval requests usually precede a chargeback.

SET

Secure Electronic Transaction, a standard that will enable secure credit card transactions on the Internet. SET will enable merchants to verify that buyers are who they claim to be.

SSL

Secure Socket Layer. A method of encryptions to secure information traveling over the Internet. SSL is now the predominant security protocol for online transactions. Messages between the merchant's server and the consumer's browser are automatically encrypted (scrambled) when sent and then decrypted (unscrambled) when received.

Settlement
The process of transferring funds for sales and credits between Acquirers and Issuers, including the final debiting of a cardholder's account and crediting a seller's account.

Shopping Cart

A software program used for Internet websites. The shopping cart totals up orders, tax, add shipping costs and transmit information to the merchant's payment gateway in order to process the sale.

Smart Card

A plastic card with an embedded microchip that can be loaded with data and used for telephone calling, electronic cash payments, or other applications.

Split Funding

A funding arrangement in which the lease company pays the equipment vendor for the leased equipment when the lease is funded.

Standard Industry Codes (SIC)

Special numbers assigned by the Card Associations to Seller types for identification and tracking purposes. MasterCard® uses MCC (Seller Category Code), while Visa® uses SIC (Standard Industry Codes).

Standard Industrial Classification

A federally designed standard system of numerical encoding by type of industry. These codes are four digit numbers used to identify business type.

Surcharges

Any additional charges to a merchant's standard processing fees. They are a result of non-qualified transactions of different communications methods.

Suspended Batch

A state in which a batch of transactions is not released to interchange because of problems noticed by the host risk system. Requires human intervention to fix the problem and settle the batch.

Swiped Card

Credit card information that is transferred by swiping or sliding the credit card through a card reader. Swiped cards are used in retail and other card-present situations. The information magnetically encoded in the magnetic stripe includes secret data that helps validate the card.

Terminated Merchant File (TMF)

Terminated Merchant File. This is a file that Visa and Mastercard contribute to in order to keep track of merchants that have funds due, excessive chargebacks, or have committed fraud.

Terminal ID (TID)

An identification number assigned to a terminal which, when sent to the download computer, identifies a group of terminal specific parameters to be sent along with the application program.

Ticket Only

A sale transaction for which a voice authorization is obtained.

Terminal

The device by which a transaction is transmitted to the acquiring bank.

Transaction Fee

A fee charged for each transaction processed by the merchant. This is in addition to the percentage discount fees.

Transaction

An act between a seller and a cardholder that results in either a paper or an electronic representation of the cardholder's promise to pay for goods or services received from the act. The action between a cardholder and a merchant that results in financial activity between the merchant and cardholder's account.

Travel and Entertainment Card (T&E)

Credit cards that typically require payment in full each month, e.g. American Express, Diner's Club, and Carte Blanche.

Triple DES (3DES)

New data encryption standard for pin pads, POS devices and ATMs adopted by the card associations.

Truncation

In ACH it normally refers to stopping or truncating a paper check as in POS or lockbox check truncation and turning that paper check into an electronic item.

Value Added Reseller (VAR)

Third party, which enhances or modifies existing hardware or software, adding value to the services provided by the processor or acquirer

Virtual Terminal

A web based credit card terminal that merchants can process sales through from any location that they have Internet access from.

Verification

The point in which the lease company verbally verifies (confirms) with the merchant that the equipment has been delivered and that they understand the lease terms in full.

VisaNet

The visa authorization and settlement systems.

Voice Authorization

A card authorization acquired via the telephone. If the transaction is approved, the merchant is provided with an authorization code (AUTHCODE) for the transaction.

Void

The reversal of an approved transaction, that has been authorized but not settled. Settled transactions require processing of a credit in order to be reversed. A void does not remove any hold on the customer's open-to-buy.

Commonly Used Acronyms

3DES	Triple DES
ACH	Automated Clearing House
AVS	Address Verification System
B2B	Business to Business
BIN	Bank Identification Number
CDPD	Cellular Digital Package Data
CVC	Card Validation Code - Mastercard
CVV2	Card Verification Value 2 - Visa
DUKPT	Derived Unique Key Per Transaction.
EBT	Electronic Benefits Transfer
ECC	Electronic Check Conversion
EDC	Electronic Draft Capture.
EMV	Europay, Mastercard, Visa
EFT	Electronic Funds Transfer
ETA	Electronic Transactions Association
FMV	Fair Market Value
GSM	Global System for Mobile Comm.
ISO	Independent Sales Organization
ISP	Industry Service Provider and Internet Service Provider
L&D Waiver	Loss and Destruction Waiver
MICR	Magnetic Ink Character Recognition
MID	Merchant Identification Number
MOTO	Mail Order Telephone Order
MSP	Merchant Service Provider
NACHA	National Automated Clearing House Association
PCS	Personal Communication System
PED	Pin Entry Devices
PIN	Personal Identification Number
POS	Point of Sale
QSR	Quick Service Restaurant
RFID	Radio Frequency Identification

RDFI	Receiving Depository Financial Institution
RP	Recurring Payment
SET	Secure Electronic Transaction
SSL	Secure Socket Layer
SIC	Standard Industry Codes
TMF	Terminated Merchant File
TID	Terminal Identification Number
T&E	Travel and Entertainment
VAR	Value Added Reseller

BIBLIOGRAPHY

Andreas, Steve & Faulkner, Charles. NLP The New Technology of Achievement. NLP Comprehensive, 1994.

Bartone, David, Esq., 1875 Eye Street, N.W., Twelfth Floor, International Square, Washington, DC 20006; Telephone: 202-223-6200; Facsimile: 202-223-6220; E-MAIL: djbartone@aol.com; website at www.lawyers.com/davidbartone

Bly, Robert. The Copywriter's Handbook (Dodd, Mead). Bly can be reached at 174 Holland Ave., New Milford, NJ 07646 - 201/599-2277.

Hogan, Kevin & Horton, William. Selling Yourself to Others The New Psychology of Sales. Gretna, LA. Pelican Publishing Company, Inc. 2002.

Gitomer, Jeffrey. The Sales Bible: The Ultimate Sales Resource. New York, NY. William Morrow, 1994.

Green, Paul. Good Selling. The Greensheet, Inc. Rohnert Park, CA, 1999.

Pittman, Bill. Developers Guide to Integrating Electronic Payments. RichSolutions, Inc, 2001.

Robbins, Anthony. Awaken The Giant Within. New York, New York. Summit Books, 1991.

Sanford, Mark, Ph.D. Fearless Cold Calling. Orinda, CA. Montaigne Publishing, 2002.

Internet Bibliography

URL:http://www.visa.com. Copyright 2002.
URL:http://www.americanexpress.com. Copyright 2002.
URL:http://www.MasterCard.com. Copyright 2002.
URL:http://www.dinersclub.com. Copyright 2002.
URL:http://www.jcbusa.com. Copyright 2002.
URL:http://www.hypercom.com. Copyright 2002.
URL:http://www.verifone.com. Copyright 2002.
URL:http://www.greensheet.com. Copyright 2002.
URL:http://www.ftc.gov. Copyright 2002.

URL:http://www.telecheck.com. Copyright 2002.
URL:http://www.epaynews.com/statistics/index.html
URL:www.ckfraud.org
URL:http://ecc.nacha.org
URL:www.electran.org
URL:www.identitytheft.org
URL:www.nacha.org
URL:www.smartcardalliance.org
URL: www.howstuffworks.com
URL:www.discoverbiz.com
URL:www.cardforum.com
URL:www.merchantfraudsquad.com
URL:www.consumer.gov/idtheft
URL:www.diogenesllc.com/checkfraud.pdf
URL:www.clev.frb.org/ccca/fo1q96/fraud.htm
URL:www.frbservices.org

Attention: Banks, Processors, Publishers, ISOs and Sales Organizations now you can join our affiliate program and earn up to 15% commissions on "How To Survive and Thrive in the Merchant Services Industry"

Just go to our site and click the affiliate program link and follow the instructions and your organization will receive your own Internet marketing link.

Just insert your link in your monthly newsletter, website or agent back office system.

You are paid a 10% commission on all sales generated and 5% commission on all affiliates that sign up from your Internet marketing link. It's a win-win.

Go to www.surviveandthrive.biz to signup now!!!

©Performance Training Systems

"He who conquers others is strong;
he who conquers himself is mighty."
— Lao-tzu